WORKPLACE VIOLENCE

WORKPLACE VIOLENCE:
BEFORE, DURING, AND AFTER

Sandra L. Heskett

Butterworth–Heinemann

Boston • Oxford • Johannesburg • Melbourne • New Delhi • Singapore

Library of Congress Cataloging-in-Publication Data

Heskett, Sandra L., 1964–
    Workplace violence: before, during, and after/Sandra L. Heskett
      p.   cm.
    Includes bibliographical references and index.
    ISBN 0-7506-9671-0
    1. Violence in the workplace. 2. Violence in the workplace —
California. I. Title.
    HF5549.5.E43H48 1996
    658.4'73–dc20
                            95-26468
                                CIP

British Library Cataloguing-in-Publication Data

A catalogue record for this book is available from the British Library.

The publisher offers special discounts on bulk orders of this book.
For information, please contact:

Manager of Special Sales
Butterworth–Heinemann
313 Washington Street
Newton, MA 02158-1626
Tel.: 617-928-2500
Fax: 617-928-2620

For information on all Security publications available, contact our
World Wide Web home page at http://www.bh.com/bh/

10 9 8 7 6 5 4 3 2 1

Printed in the United States of America

*This book is dedicated to the thousands of people
who have lost their lives because of workplace violence and
to the people who can work to prevent future violence.
Actions can make a difference.*

Contents

Foreword

I was visiting the human relations director of a small manufacturing company last month, and the first thing that I noticed was that he had rearranged his furniture. When I asked him about the new layout, he explained that an employee who had just had her hours cut had stormed into his office and essentially trapped him between his desk and the wall. The incident ended without injury when the employee got tired of yelling and just left. The director explained that by setting his desk in the middle of the room, he would now have an escape route available if a similar incident ever occurred.

I told him that he was indeed lucky to have escaped injury and that it was probably wise to rearrange the furniture. I then asked him, "What else are you doing to prevent workplace violence?" and got a blank stare in return. It was obvious that, other than taking steps to protect himself, this "professional people person" had no idea that anything else could be done.

This book is designed to meet the needs of all businesspeople who find that they have to confront workplace violence. The current business emphasis on productivity and efficiency often overlooks the fact that employees are indeed human and, as human beings, have the capacity for violence. Mergers, downsizing, and "right-sizing" may be advantageous for the chief executive officers and the stockholders, but they create tremendous stress among employees. Add to this the everyday stress of living in the nineties—developing relationships, raising a family, budgeting in an economy in which each paycheck seems to be worth less—and it's surprising that more violent events don't occur.

In her book, Sandra Heskett gives us a realistic look at the problems of workplace violence. She then provides guidance on preventing violence and regaining control over the workplace. This book should be required reading for human relations, occupational safety, and physical security professionals. All business owners, managers, and supervisors should also read this book. Ms. Heskett's personal experiences add credibility to her words and create a usable, straightforward book that can help us confront this real and immediate issue.

Chuck Goodman
Training Manager
Iowa-Illinois Safety Council

Preface

June 18, 1991, was in many ways a very significant day for me. It was on this day that I reported to work in my new position as security supervisor for a large firm in Iowa. After working my way up through the ranks of security personnel and completing my college degree, I felt very positive about my professional future. There were about eight hundred people employed at my company, and I knew most of them by name.

On that day, I proudly set up my new office and accepted the congratulations of my coworkers. All was going well until I received a telephone call and was told that a gunman had walked into an affiliate office in Jacksonville, Florida, and embarked on a bloody rampage. I would not understand the significance of that telephone call for a long time to come.

Why had this happened? It turned out that the assailant's car had been repossessed earlier. He had been late making his payments and was upset that the finance company had taken this action. He killed eight people and wounded five more. This tragedy made front-page headlines across the United States and sent shock waves across the country.

Even though the rampage took place over a thousand miles away and I did not personally know any of the people involved, the tragedy struck home. Employees at the office where I worked were grief-stricken for people they had never met. The incident was painful as we listened to the gruesome details. Employees feared for their own safety, and many no longer felt safe at the workplace. They immediately became extremely concerned about building security. They wanted guaranteed protection, and they wanted it now.

A group of employees demanded that metal detectors be installed at every door, that the reception area be contained in bullet-proof glass, and that visitors, customers, and family members be searched for weapons as they entered the facility.

When I got home that evening, I received numerous telephone calls, only one of which I remember in great detail. The call came from Jacksonville, Florida, where the killings had taken place. Because Jacksonville is a large town with thousands of offices and buildings, I had not made any connection between family members who lived in Jacksonville and the murders that had taken place there. A telephone call from my twin sister, Deb, changed that and brought the shootings to a personal level. Deb had been working just a few blocks away at a video rental store when the shooting took place. As she told me of the murders and the hysteria that had seized the town, I felt very sad for the victims and their families.

This tragedy took eight lives. It robbed many people of their children, parents, siblings, and friends. It raised my awareness of the growing epidemic of workplace violence, and it helped inspire me to write this book.

ACKNOWLEDGMENTS

The first and foremost acknowledgment must be to my parents, Ardella Heskett and Floyd and Alicia Heskett. In a hundred lifetimes I would never be able to repay them for their wisdom and patience. The gifts they gave me will last a lifetime. I'll love them forever.

I would also like to acknowledge the following people for their contributions: Arlin Ciechanowski, Betty Getty, Chuck Goodman, Pastor Arno Melz, Leon Mosley, Mr. and Mrs. Norbin Meyer, Dr. Barbara Murphy, Larry "Nick" Nicholson, Bob Rendl, Vince Rodriguez, Dick Studdard, Amy Ward, Ken Wernimont, Deb Wood, a special lady named Cathy, and a fine man named John. Each of these people contributed their time, effort, support, and knowledge to this project.

Thanks to the many others who helped with this manuscript. I hope they realize who they are. I'll never forget. Without their support and assistance, this project would not have been possible.

A final and most meaningful dedication goes to my brother, Walter Corey Heskett. Corey helped teach me the meaning of true excellence, being true and committed to my beliefs, and, most important, unconditional love. (Corey, you've always been my idol, and, Corey, this one's for you.)

Introduction

You cannot escape the responsibility of tomorrow by
evading it today.

—Abraham Lincoln

On Monday, June 20, 1994, Dean Mellberg, recently discharged
from the U.S. Air Force for emotional problems, left his hotel room
and sat quietly on a curb waiting for a taxi. Next to Mellberg was
a large gym bag. The taxi took Mellberg ten miles to the Fairchild
Air Force Hospital in Spokane, Washington. Once there, Mellberg
began a violent and bloody rampage that took him and his Chinese-
made MAK-90 into specific offices, down corridors, into the hospital cafeteria, and eventually out onto the hospital lawn.

The massacre ended when a military policeman on a bicycle
shot and killed Mellberg. The death toll in the incident was five,
with twenty-three others injured. Among those killed was Major
Thomas Brigham, the psychiatrist who, along with other mental-
health professionals, had recommended that Mellberg be discharged. An eight-year-old girl sitting in the hospital cafeteria was
also killed. The next day, eight victims remained in critical condition, including a four-year-old boy and a five-year-old girl.

Most of the people injured or killed at the air force hospital
had never met Mellberg. They were family members of military
personnel stationed at the base, and it was just by chance that they
happened to be at the hospital at the time of the shooting.

The trauma and tragedy unfolded the next day in front-page
headlines all across America. Millions of people read the articles

or saw the news on television. The reports continued for some time as the details of the killing spree became known and the countless questions were answered.

As employees and employers, we have our own questions, which typically go unanswered. Probably the most common question is, Why did this happen? Other questions include, Am I, or my company, at risk for this type of tragedy? What can be done? How can I tell if an employee in my firm is at the point of believing that violence is the answer?

The truth is that there are no perfect, clear-cut answers. There are, however, specific indicators of potentially violent incidents, and there are established guidelines for protecting employees, customers, and organizations. That information is contained in this book.

Today, workplace intimidation, threats, physical assault, and homicide are issues that every business and worker must address. Incidents of violence in the workplace have increased so dramatically that the Centers for Disease Control now considers occupational violence to be a serious public health problem.[1]

In September 1993, the National Institute for Occupational Safety and Health (NIOSH) released an alert stating that workers in certain industries and occupations were at increased risk of homicide. This statement was based on the results of a comprehensive study on violence in the workplace between 1980 to 1989. During that period, NIOSH found that homicide was the third leading cause of workplace death for all workers. Only motor vehicle accidents and machine-related incidents topped violence as the cause of death. NIOSH also found that homicide was the leading cause of death for women in the workplace. Homicide accounted for approximately 7,600 workplace deaths, or 12 percent of the total, during the eighties. Firearms were used in 75 percent of the homicides, and knives and similar weapons were used in 14 percent.

Since the NIOSH alert was released, occupational homicide has increased. In 1994, the Bureau of Labor Statistics announced that workplace homicide was the second leading cause of occupational homicide in the United States.[2]

The release of the NIOSH alert generated a furor of concern among regulatory agencies and private businesses alike. The days when "ignorance was bliss" were gone forever. The increased threat of violence in their organizations challenged human resource managers, safety managers, and security managers to identify, examine, and eradicate the risks that their organizations face. They needed measures to prevent bloodshed in their workplaces. Meanwhile, newspaper headlines all across the United States continued to narrate stories of fatal robberies, bombings, and murderous former employees.

The legal and social environments in which businesses operate have changed drastically over the past few years. The Occupational Health and Safety Administration (OSHA) has begun to cite employers who have not adequately addressed and dealt with threats of violence or harassment issues, resulting in costly fines. Companies and individuals can be held legally and criminally liable for failing to provide a safe, secure, and healthful work environment for their employees. Case law has awarded multimillion-dollar settlements to victims and their families when companies failed to provide security for their employees. The direction of the courts is clear: Companies must address workplace security issues now or pay severely later.

The prevention of aggressive and violent behavior is not a simple matter. Violence in the workplace is not committed by a specific category of people. Those who commit violence include employees (former and current), their friends and family members, customers, vendors, felons, and other criminals.

Violence is possible in every type of workplace. Often the nature of and motivation for the violence are directly related to the establishment's characteristics and the services offered. For example, retail trade and services are the occupations that have the highest rate of workplace homicide. One motive in a significant number of these incidents is robbery. When the likelihood of a robbery occurring is reduced, the overall likelihood of occupational homicide is also reduced.

Researchers and professional security writers have focused on using behavioral red flags, warning signs, and generic profiles to identify potential employee offenders. Researchers have devised a profile for the "typical" offender. However, caution must be exercised when using this profile. Those who typecast certain employees may overlook others who harbor a propensity for violence but do not fit the profile.

To understand the perspective of the potential offender, we must first understand human behavior as it relates to the relationship between individuals and their work. Social and economic considerations have played an important role in the increase of violence in the workplace. It may be that in our culture workplace violence is more acceptable than it was twenty years ago, or perhaps after reading about violence almost every day, we have become desensitized to it.

Looking beyond the individual, businesses must examine themselves to identify any factors that make their workplaces conducive to violence. Company policies and procedures, security measures, hiring practices, disciplinary procedures, and the effectiveness of employee-assistance programs must be measured.

The thoroughness of a company's planning can determine its ability to survive following a violent incident. Acts of violence committed in the workplace can vary greatly in both their severity and their impact on an organization. The effects can last from days to years. The biggest impact is the human anguish with which surviving employees are left to deal. In some cases, counseling by mental-health professionals can last for years, and some victims never fully regain their previous level of mental health and well-being.

Not every company has the resources available to provide a full-time, on-site security staff. The next best thing is to examine how the company can make the most of the resources it already has. Many options are available that do not cost tremendous amounts of money. The information in this book will assist small-business owners who do not have the resources of the large corporations.

Written policies and procedures can help companies deter violence. A written recovery strategy can help companies identify, evaluate, control, and resolve potentially volatile situations when they arise. The time spent today on planning may later determine the extent of the effects of violence on the business, its employees and customers, and the community.

REFERENCES

1. U.S. Department of Health and Human Services, Centers for Disease Control and Prevention, *Alert: Request for Assistance in Preventing Homicides in the Workplace* (Washington, D.C.: U.S. Government Printing Office, 1993).
2. U.S. Department of Labor, Bureau of Labor Statistics, *News* (Washington, D.C.: U.S. Government Printing Office, 1994.)

I

Aspects of Workplace Violence

1

Introduction to Violence in the Workplace

Times are changing. When we look at the history of the United States, it's readily apparent that more changes have occurred in the past thirty years than in the previous two hundred years. In the past thirty years, we have sent humans to the moon, developed airplanes capable of sending hundreds of people thousands of miles in a few short hours, and invented methods of instant communication via satellites, fax machines, and mobile telephones. On a more personal level, think of the differences between the toys you played with as a child and the toys your children or grandchildren are playing with today. Thanks to technology, dolls are now capable of talking back and developing interactive stories.

The effect of all of these changes is phenomenal. To put it bluntly, we're not the same society we were ten or twenty years ago. These rapid changes have affected the very fabric of our lives in both positive and negative ways.

For example, one benefit of rapid communication is faster access to information and news. We can sit in our easy chairs and watch the Olympics live and cheer with the rest of the nation as our proud athletes compete for world recognition and honors. Millions of people watched in astonishment as the Berlin Wall fell, witnessing the effect this had on others thousands of miles away.

Other, less positive, effects of recent changes include having our parents, children, siblings, and other family members move to other parts of the country or world. With these changes, little of the "Leave It to Beaver" family atmosphere remains. Our natural family support groups have diminished. People today often feel alone and isolated from the rest of the world. Many people don't know their neighbors' names and really don't care about them as long as they don't have a dog that barks constantly at three o'clock in the morning. Crime rates have increased noticeably as well. Figure 1–1 shows the change in nonlethal crime statistics in the United States between 1973 and 1992.

Both positive and negative changes have also occurred in the work force. On the positive side, more managerial classes are offered today, and we're slowly moving away from the authoritarian management style toward focused work groups and team-based philosophies. Ball-and-chain management styles are being replaced with team concepts, and work and family issues are finally being addressed. Few employee-assistance programs existed twenty years ago, but now they play an intregral role in many larger corporations. Companies are beginning to recognize the value of their employees as part of their real assets. The Americans with Disabilities Act now requires employers to make modifications or reasonable accommodations for the special needs of their employees.

On the negative side, layoffs are an everyday occurrence. Call it "downsizing" or "right-sizing" or whichever term you like, the results are the same. People are losing their jobs by the thousands. The majority of the workers in the United States who have not lost their jobs due to a layoff know family members or close friends who have. Even those who are not directly affected still experience

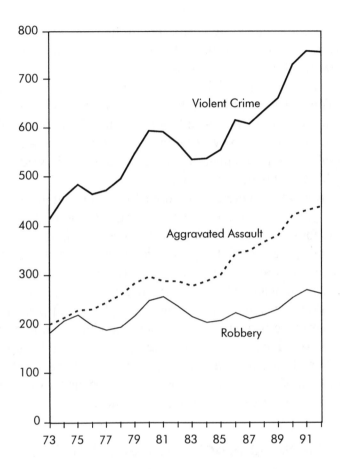

Figure 1–1   Index of nonlethal crime in the United States, 1973–1993.

the indirect effects of layoffs or job terminations. Relocation to other cities for other jobs takes family members and friends away. This erodes a person's support network.

Workers see their friends and families struggle to make ends meet as they slowly sell off possessions to avoid losing their homes. Savings accounts that took a lifetime to build up are quickly spent. They can't even hope to replace the retirement or college money that took years of struggling to acquire. Somewhere in the back of most people's minds is a fear that it could happen to them.

This is true for the majority of workers in the United States. Most of us can become a statistic in the blink of an eye, and it can happen tomorrow. Life has indeed changed.

Twenty years ago, a job loss was a traumatic event for most people. The newly unemployed might spend a day or two grieving or brooding over the job loss and then get busy filling out applications with potential employers. After a day, a week, or a month, they usually found a comparable job at a comparable wage with comparable benefits. Life went on.

Today's job market does not offer the same guarantees. It is more competitive than ever before. There are often fifty to 250 applicants for every "good" job available. The jobs that are readily available are part-time or temporary jobs that pay close to minimum wage and offer few or no benefits. These types of positions usually seem demeaning to workers who are accustomed to a wage of fifteen dollars per hour and a cafeteria-style benefit plan. They believe that these types of jobs are more suitable for kids paying their way through college than for wage earners trying to support a family. In addition, automation is replacing manual labor. Job loss and the threat of job loss are just two of the reasons for the alarming increase in incidents of workplace violence.

HIGH-RISK WORKPLACES AND OCCUPATIONS

Given the ongoing publicity, it may seem surprising that the U.S. Postal Service does not have the highest rate of workplace homicide. In fact, the U.S. Postal Service does not even make the top-ten list. Although post office murders attract a great deal of attention, the Postal Service has a lower homicide rate than the national average.

When the National Institute for Occupational Safety and Health (NIOSH) calculates the incident rates for workplaces, the formula used is based on the number of homicides per one hundred thousand workers. Workplaces are defined according to the *Standard Industry Classification (SIC) Manual.* The simple formula is as follows:

Number of homicides per SIC code ÷ number of employees per SIC code

The larger the number of employees, the lower the ratio of employees to homicides. Because the U.S. Postal Service is the third largest employer in the United States, the division reduces the end result number.

The NIOSH alert issued in September 1993 listed the workplaces with the highest rates of occupational violence between 1980 and 1989. They are listed in Table 1–1. The occupations with the highest rates of occupational violence during this period, according to the same NIOSH alert, are listed in Table 1–2.

Another study published by the Centers for Disease Control looked at the causes of occupational deaths in various industries between 1980 and 1989. The findings of this study are shown in Table 1–3, which compares violence to other causes of death in the workplace.

The following risk factors are associated with workplace violence:

- Exchanging money
- Working alone at night and during early morning hours
- Having money, valued items, jewelry, or other items that are easily exchanged for cash available
- Performing public safety functions in the community
- Working with patients, clients, or customers known to have or suspected of having a history of violence
- Working with employees with a history of assaults or who exhibit belligerent, intimidating, or threatening behavior toward others

THE STATISTICS

Statistics can be fascinating. They are available on almost every subject you can imagine. Whether you are interested in the number of births in your county in a given year or the number of fish caught at a local pond in 1978, you can probably find the answer buried in your library somewhere. Statistical analysis is a combi-

Table 1–1   Workplaces with the highest levels of occupational violence, 1980–1989.

Workplace	Number of Workplace Homicides	Rate per 100,000
Taxicab establishment	287	26.9
Liquor store	115	8.0
Gas station	304	5.6
Detective/protection service	152	5.0
Justice and public order	640	3.4
Grocery store	806	3.2
Jewelry store	56	3.2
Hotel/motel	153	1.5
Eating and drinking establishment	734	1.5

Source: U.S. Department of Health and Human Services, Centers for Disease Control and Prevention, *Alert: Request for Assistance in Preventing Homicides in the Workplace* (Washington, D.C.: U.S. Government Printing Office, 1993), p. 3.

Table 1–2   Occupations with the highest levels of occupational violence, 1980–1989.

Occupation	Number of Occupational Homicides	Rate per 100,000
Taxicab driver/chauffeur	289	15.1
Law enforcement officer	520	9.3
Hotel clerk	40	5.1
Gas station worker	164	4.5
Security officer	253	3.6
Stock handler/bagger	260	3.1
Store owner/manager	1,065	2.8
Bartender	84	2.1

Source: U.S. Department of Health and Human Services, Centers for Disease Control and Prevention, *Alert: Request for Assistance in Preventing Homicides in the Workplace* (Washington, D.C.: U.S. Government Printing Office, 1993), p. 4.

Table 1-3 Average annual rate (per 100,000 workers) of traumatic occupational fatalities by cause of death and industry division in the United States, 1980–1989.

Cause of Death	Total*	Mining	Constr.	Manuf.	T/C/PU†	Whlsle	Retail	Fin./Ins.	Service	Pub.Admin.
Motor vehicle	1.61	5.27	3.72	0.62	11.44	0.93	0.39	0.3	0.54	1.87
Machine	0.95	7.39	3.5	0.85	1.24	0.26	0.09	0.1	0.19	0.28
Homicide	0.85	0.48	0.65	0.27	1.47	0.19	1.66	0.39	0.61	1.54
Falls	0.67	1.89	6.56	0.36	0.85	0.17	0.11	0.13	0.26	0.27
Electrocution	0.50	2.27	3.99	0.25	1.45	0.09	0.05	0.03	0.14	0.16
Falling object	0.46	4.33	1.95	0.64	0.7	0.1	0.06	0.02	0.13	0.13
Air transportation	0.29	0.66	0.18	0.08	2.00	0.07	0.03	0.1	0.15	1.06
Suicide	0.22	0.15	0.36	0.12	0.29	0.09	0.18	0.15	0.23	0.28
Explosion	0.19	2.46	0.53	0.25	0.36	0.09	0.04	0.008	0.09	0.09

Source: U.S. Department of Health and Human Services, Centers for Disease Control and Prevention, *Fatal Injuries to Workers in the United States, 1980–1989: A Decade of Surveillance* (August 1993).

*Totals include cases for which industry could not be classified (7%). Several risk factors have been identified that contribute to the likelihood of violence occurring in the workplace. Managers and business owners can use knowledge of these risk factors to reduce the incidence of violence in their establishments. A correlation between these risk factors and the workplaces and occupations with the highest rates of homicide reveals a definite relationship between variables. Retail trade and services are the occupations with the highest rates of workplace homicide.

†Transportation/Communication/Public Utilities

nation of art and science. Much of the validity of the statistics depends on the people completing the research.

Knowing the numbers alone will not stop or prevent violence; the numbers serve only as a means of looking at the past and predicting future events in a given set of circumstances. The tables and figures in this chapter are valuable in that they show crime trends based on various factors.

To gain insight into the extent of workplace violence, the statistics need to be compared to crime in the United States as a whole. A comparison of the increase in violent crimes in general and the increase in violent acts in the workplace shows that incidents of workplace violence are increasing more rapidly than most other crimes. Crime trend data reveal a comprehensive scope of workplace violence.

Crime in the United States is undoubtedly on the rise. According to the "crime clocks" formulated by the *Uniform Crime Reports*, in 1962 a forcible rape was committed every thirty-two minutes in the United States; in 1992, a forcible rape was committed every five minutes.[1] Other comparisons between crime rates in 1962 and 1992 are listed in Table 1–4. The time frames listed by the *Uniform Crime Reports* represent the annual ratio of crime in the United States to fixed time intervals.

According to the *Uniform Crime Reports*, the incidence of murder has increased 23 percent from 1983 to 1992. Total violent crimes (murder, forcible rape, robbery, and aggravated assault) climbed 53.6 percent during the same period. Occupational homicide is growing at a much faster rate than the other categories of murder. Because record keeping on occupational homicides is relatively new, few actual figures are available, and the increase can only be estimated. For California, there was a 22.6 percent increase in occupational homicides in just one year (1992–1993).

According to the 1993 Census of Fatal Occupational Injuries, 1,063 people died on the job as a result of work-related homicides. The majority of these homicides occurred during a robbery or other crime. Robberies and miscellaneous crimes accounted for 793 (75 percent) of the 1,063 occupational deaths in 1993. The next

Table 1–4   Crime in the United States, 1962 and 1992.

Crime	1962	1992
Aggravated assault	4 minutes	28 seconds
Burglary	35 seconds	11 seconds
Larceny theft	1 minute	11 seconds
Motor vehicle theft	90 seconds	4 seconds
Murder	60 minutes	22 minutes
Rape	32 minutes	5 minutes
Robbery	6 minutes	47 seconds

Source: U.S. Department of Justice, *Uniform Crime Reports: Crime in the United States* (Washington, D.C.: U.S. Government Printing Office, 1963), p. 14; and *Uniform Crime Reports*, 3 October 1993, p. 58.

largest category of job-related homicides were those committed by work-related associates—106 (10 percent) of the deaths. Of these, 59 occurred at the hands of a current or former coworker. In the rest of the work-related homicides, 43 murders were committed by customers or clients. Personal acquaintances accounted for 4 percent; police officers, 6 percent; and security guards, 5 percent of occupational homicides. The motives involved in the remaining 4 work-associated deaths were not specified. The number of murders committed by work associates could easily be twice as high; many of these crimes might be reported as other criminal acts. For example, if one employee kills another outside of the work environment, the murder might not be classified as a work-related homicide.

NORMAL VERSUS ABNORMAL HUMAN BEHAVIOR

Why do we react the way we do in a given set of circumstances? Chances are, at one time or another we've all acted in a way that surprised even ourselves. There are times when "the devil made me do it" is our only defense. What makes us act the way we do?

Most of the time, we try to act like the responsible, caring people that we want to be. We treat our friends well, otherwise they wouldn't be our friends. We love our spouses, try to get along with our coworkers, attend services at a house of worship, sometimes give time and money to charities, and refrain from beating the dog.

Once in a while, though, we argue with our spouse, clash with our boss, and yell at the dog. We know we're not perfect, but we like to think we're good people. We like to think the same of our friends and family.

Then as we sit down to watch the evening news, we see the trial of a mother who murdered her two children by drowning them in a car. Everybody who listens to the gruesome details of the deaths is emotionally affected. People worry because they fear for their own children; they turn away in disgust. We ask ourselves how this could happen and what kind of person could this mother be. Advocates of the death penalty appear to be everywhere.

The news anchor then shows video from the latest court developments in a celebrity trial. The next news story talks about a gang-related drive-by shooting in which three kids were killed. The next report is about a big drug bust. The following news piece tells of overcrowding at the local jail. The kind feelings we had half an hour ago give way to the suspicion that we are stuck in the middle of a sick society.

We question how people can commit such acts of violence against others. We know sooner or later that these crimes will spread from other people's neighborhoods into our own. We consider how long it will be before the armed desperado comes into our office, our home, our life, and opens fire. We dread the thought of our own parents, children, brothers, sisters, aunts, and uncles becoming victims.

Again we wonder what it is that makes a person act in a certain way. Once a fellow security officer told me that everybody out there is fighting their own form of mental illness. In the years since, I have reflected on that thought numerous times. I think the statement was more perceptive than even the security officer intended. I suspect each of us has ghosts in our closet and feelings we would never dare to share with others. Maybe understanding our own feelings and fears and their origins can help us comprehend the behavior of others. By looking at the environment in which we operate, perhaps we can see ways that we can improve society.

Even on the most difficult day, though, few of us would consider using violence as the means to an end. Not all people affected by stress will turn to violence, and not all forms of mental illness lead to violence. *Abnormal behavior* is a broad term that can describe conditions relative to mental illness, alcohol intoxication, drug-induced impairments, and stress-related disorders. This is only a partial listing of the causes of abnormal behavior.

Due to diversity among people and among cultures, it's difficult to describe what might be considered abnormal behavior. In one set of circumstances, a certain behavior may be totally appropriate, whereas the same actions would be considered abnormal elsewhere.

One way to think about normal versus abnormal behavior is to think about what the reasonable person might expect in a particular set of circumstances. For the most part, this parallels the way our judicial system works. When trying to figure out if an employee's behavior would be considered normal, evaluate what the reasonable person would do. Keep in mind that the reasonable person is somebody who is both like and unlike the typical manager or supervisor. The reasonable person may not have the same heritage, background, values, or goals as every other person. What may seem totally inconceivable to one person may seem perfectly normal to another. Diversity exists in the workplace, and the amount of diversity will grow and continue to be a powerful characteristic of the workplace in the future.

Imagine for a moment that all of your employees are invited to a company-sponsored picnic. Each employee is to bring a side dish to accompany the hamburgers supplied by the company. Depending on the diversity in the workplace, you might expect to see all kinds of ethnic foods. What about the employee who brings a steaming dish of dog food? Most people would consider this abnormal.

Now consider how the reasonable person would respond to conflict in the workplace. With this example it might be harder to give an exact answer because people react differently. One person might cry, another might withdraw socially, and another might quit. Under any set of circumstances, it would not be normal to threaten violence against oneself or another. This behavior is just not appropriate in the workplace. In this day and age, it would not be considered reasonable to think that violence, in any form, should be used when dealing with conflict or stress. Employees who do use threatening or intimidating actions to "win" need to be dealt with.

REFERENCES

1. U.S. Department of Justice, *Uniform Crime Reports: Crime in the United States* (Washington, D.C.: U.S. Government Printing Office, October 3, 1993), p. 4.

2

Forms of Violence

When business owners and managers think about violence in the workplace, they often visualize a former employee brandishing a handgun. This type of workplace violence represents only a small number of the actual cases that occur. Robberies, assaults, rapes, and verbal abuse occur much more frequently. On any given day in the United States, hundreds of people become the victims of less publicized incidents of workplace violence.

According to a survey conducted by the Society of Human Resource Managers (SHRM) in 1993, 44 percent of the companies surveyed reported that acts of violence had occurred in the workplace that year; 29.6 percent reported between three and five incidents of violence in the workplace during the past five years.[1]

Violent crimes are committed against employees for a variety of reasons. An examination of the motivation for violence in the workplace can indicate the types of violence that might affect various occupations. An investigation into the victim/offender relationship can help determine which employees are at risk.

MOTIVATIONS FOR VIOLENCE

In 1994, the California Division of Occupational Safety and Health Administration (CAL/OSHA) issued a set of guidelines developed to reduce incidents of workplace violence.[2] It is widely believed that the federal Occupational Safety and Health Administration will mirror these guidelines when developing national standards. (CAL/OSHA's guidelines are covered in Chapter 10.) In the guidelines, violent incidents in the workplace are divided into three types of events. (See the box "CAL/OSHA's Major Types of Workplace Violence."). These categories are based on the relationship, if any, of the offender with the victim of the crime or the workplace where the crime occurred. CAL/OSHA recommends specific security measures to guard against each type of violence. Occupations may be subject to more than one type of violence.

In Type I incidents, the offender does not have a legitimate relationship with employees or with the business itself. The motive for this category is robbery or another act of violence. This category represents the majority of workplace homicides that occur in California. In most of these incidents, the criminal enters a small retail establishment late at night with the intention of robbing the attendant. During the course of the robbery, the attendant, often the owner, is killed.

The following risk factors are present during this type of incident:

- The business exchanges money with customers.
- Few employees are present at a time.
- The business operates at night or early in the morning.
- Employees have face-to-face contact with customers.

Businesses with the highest incident rate in this category include gas stations, convenience stores, liquor stores, and similar businesses. Security officers, janitorial staff, and taxi drivers killed while on duty are included in this category. Many of these incidents occur in an almost random fashion. The act of violence is often unpredictable and unforeseeable. Criminals most likely pick their

CAL/OSHA's Major Types of Workplace Violence

Type I

The offender does not have a legitimate relationship with the business or its employees. Robbery is often the motive. This category represents the majority of cases of work-related violence. Typical victims include the following:

- Convenience and liquor store employees
- Taxicab drivers
- Restaurant and grocery store employees
- Hotel and motel clerks

Type II

The victim is a service provider, and the assailant is a recipient of those services. The following are the typical victims of this type of violence:

- Police and public safety professionals
- Medical care providers
- Social workers
- Attorneys and judges

Type III

The assailant has some sort of relationship with the business or an employee. Typical assailants in this type of violence include the following:

- Current or former employees
- Current or former friends of employees
- Relatives of employees
- Current or former customers

targets based on which businesses are the most convenient or are the easiest to victimize. Employees who know what to look for have a much better opportunity of predicting potentially threatening situations.

The victims of Type II incidents are service providers. While fulfilling their job-related responsibilities, they are victimized as a result of the type of service they provide. Police officers and others employed in law enforcement and corrections are prime candidates for violence directed toward them in the course of employment. Besides law enforcement and corrections, other occupations are at risk for Type II violence:

- Medical-care providers
- Mental-heath providers
- Alcohol- and drug-treatment employees
- Correctional facility employees
- Social workers in almost every field
- Justice system employees, including judges and attorneys
- Other public safety professionals

For workers who fit into Type II occupations, the threat of violence is almost a daily occurrence. According to CAL/OSHA, Type II violence is increasing. In terms of nonfatal injuries to workers, this category of violence may be the most widespread.

In Type III incidents, the assailant has some type of relationship with either an employee or the business. The assailant could be a current or former employee seeking revenge against another employee, a supervisor or manager, or the establishment itself. The offender could be the current or former spouse or lover of an employee. Other examples of crimes in this category include violent acts at the workplace in which the victim and the offender have a relationship external to the workplace. Stalking cases that end violently at the work site are classified as Type III incidents.

Occurrences of Type III violence typically attract a great deal of media attention. One reason for this might be that no matter who you are or where you work, you really can't know, with any degree of certainty, if another employee is on the verge of committing a violent act at your workplace. People can readily see themselves as potential victims. Employees can only speculate about the emotional well-being of coworkers and, in some cases, their families. The media has almost created a panic among workers.

Almost unheard of ten years ago, Type III incidents are increasing at an alarming rate. It's impossible to escape the stories of former employees and disgruntled workers returning to the work site in a violent manner. Murders within the U.S. Postal Service have made headlines from coast to coast. Although Type III incidents might not cause the most occupational homicides, managers and supervisors would be extremely foolish to believe that it could never happen at their work site. The good news is that managers and supervisors do have some control over the Type III incidents occurring at their work site.

Verbal abuse, assaults, and rapes occurring among coworkers are far more common than occupational homicides. Because these acts of violence are greatly underreported, the extent of abuse can only be estimated. According to the National Crime Victimization Survey conducted in 1992 by the Bureau of Justice Statistics, 11 percent of all violent crimes are work related. The bureau estimates that 670,000 workers were assaulted (simple assault, aggravated assault, robbery, and rape) while at work or while on duty in 1992.[3]

The relationships that exist among coworkers and between management and employees can be instrumental in determining a particular business's risk of workplace violence. Training and education are key factors in the prevention of Type III incidents. Many preventive and security measures can be used to protect against each type of violence; they are covered in Chapter 6. The CAL/ OSHA guidelines for preventing violence in the workplace are summarized in Chapter 10.

INTERNAL CRIMES AGAINST THE COMPANY

Violence can take many forms, each varying in intensity and potential destructive behavior. Whereas some acts of violence are committed against people, many other acts are committed against equipment, products, or data, to name just a few. Acts that the perpetrator might view as only mildly destructive can have extremely harmful effects on the company as a whole.

The financial stability of almost any company can be severely damaged with a few carefully placed keystrokes. Companies have been crippled and even closed by a disgruntled employee who seeks revenge for something as simple as the discontinuation of the annual Christmas bonus.

Sabotage that forces a business to close its doors obviously has far-reaching and devastating effects on employees, business owners (including stockholders, who may include the majority of employees), customers, and the community. Pharmaceutical companies that have experienced product tampering by employees have had to spend millions of dollars in tamperproof containers, not to speak of the millions sunk into litigation and settlements. They may never regain customer confidence. Companies that have experienced the end result of sabotage can readily see why product or service integrity is such a vital part of the overall company mission statement.

Destructive acts of violence by an employee or customer can start on a small scale; the damage is often blamed on carelessness, accidents, the normal breakdown of equipment, and a host of other causes. The true origin of the damage is rarely determined. Supervisors and managers who are busy trying to meet production quotas or keep up with daily tasks might overlook the incident rather than spend countless hours conducting an investigation that they believe will most likely lead to a dead end.

DRUG ABUSE IN THE WORKPLACE

Abuse of legal and illegal drugs by employees both on and off the job is increasing. The implications of this increase are devastating to U.S. businesses. The costs associated with drug abuse are astonishing. According to the U.S. Department of Health and Human Services, which conducted an extensive study in the mid-eighties on the economic costs associated with alcohol and drug abuse and mental illness, alcohol abuse had an economic cost of $70.3 billion in 1985. The economic cost of drug abuse was estimated at $44.1 billion, and mental illness had an estimated $103.7 billion impact on the U.S. economy.[4]

In 1985, crimes associated with alcohol and drug abuse and mental illness resulted in prison sentences totaling an estimated 232,530 years. Using eighty as the average human life span, this amounts to 2,907 lives wasted in one year alone. Alcohol abuse accounted for nearly 68 percent of those wasted lives. Premature deaths attributable to alcohol or drug abuse or mental illness totaled 140,593 in one year alone.

The future trends on abuse are even more grim when we consider that the high school students of today will be the workers of tomorrow. In a survey of twelfth graders in 1993, 62.5 percent of the respondents reporting having been drunk at some point in their life. An astonishing 72 percent reported using alcohol in the past thirty days. In the same study, 42.9 percent reported using illicit drugs, including marijuana, hallucinogens, cocaine, heroin, stimulants, barbiturates, and tranquilizers not prescribed by a doctor.[5] Many of these twelfth graders have already entered the work force. The graduating high school classes in the past decade are very familiar with drug and alcohol abuse among their friends and peers. Figure 2–1 shows the extent of illicit drug use among young adults.

Clearly, drug and alcohol abuse are problems encountered at all workplaces throughout the United States. The abuse has become so widespread that supervisors are required to undergo training to detect symptoms and signs indicative of drug and alcohol abuse among employees who drive vehicles on the job. This law, the Omnibus Employee Testing Act, requires drivers to submit to an alcohol or controlled substance test when the employer has reasonable suspicion that the driver is in violation of alcohol or controlled substance regulations. The Omnibus Employee Testing Act states:

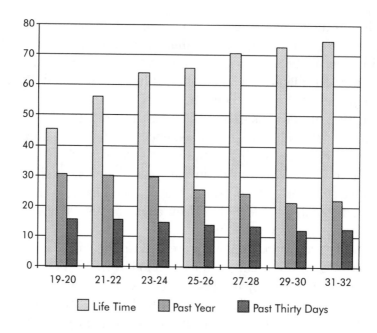

Figure 2–1 Illicit drug use among ages 19–32, stated as a percentage of age group population.

Each employer shall ensure that persons designated to determine whether reasonable suspicion exists to require a driver to undergo testing receive at least 60 minutes of training on alcohol misuse and receive at least an additional 60 minutes of training on controlled substances use. The training shall cover physical, behavioral, speech and performance indicators of probable alcohol misuse and use of controlled substances.

The aim of the training is to give supervisors the tools they need to identify potential problem employees. Once an employee has been identified as a possible substance abuser, the supervisor has a responsibility to monitor job behavior and performance. The employer must require a driver to submit to alcohol or controlled substance testing when reasonable suspicion has been established. The employer must also require additional testing when the employee returns to work from a substance abuse program and periodically thereafter.

The intention of this law is to prevent employees who are misusing alcohol or controlled substances from injuring themselves or other people. The supervisor must also act in accordance with company policies regarding workplace safety and substance abuse.

Although not every company is subject to this regulation, training on drug abuse is a valuable tool for all supervisors, managers, and employees in the battle to curb workplace violence. According to a survey conducted by Northwestern National Life Insurance Company and published by *EAP Digest* in 1994, 59 percent of U.S. workers believe that alcohol and drug abuse is a factor in workplace violence.[6]

Employees who are abusing or misusing alcohol or controlled substances are more likely to have performance problems than their peers. Managers and supervisors need to know how to deal with abusers. Ignoring the behavioral or performance problems associated with the abuse will only postpone inevitable counseling or disciplinary actions. (See the box "Signs of Drug Misuse in the Workplace.") Because part of the employee's problem includes denial, the problem is likely to continue to grow without the intervention of a third party, such as the employer.

> Employees with a drinking problem are absent 16 times more than the average employee, have an accident rate that is 4 times higher, use one-third more sickness benefits and have 5 times more compensation claims while on the job. Forty percent of industrial fatalities and 47 percent of industrial injuries can be traced to alcohol abuse.[7]

The supervisor who has reasonable cause to believe that an employee is either physically or mentally impaired as the result of substance abuse needs to respond in a manner that minimizes the potential danger associated with the impairment while maximizing the safety of others with whom the impaired employee may come in contact. Each company should have an alcohol- and substance-abuse policy that provides guidance and support to the supervisory

Signs of Drug Misuse in the Workplace

Attendance
Tardiness arriving for work
Tardiness returning from lunch
Leaving workplace
Frequent absences
Missed appointments
Absences from work

Quality of Work
Increased mistakes
Lack of attention/concentration
Difficulty recalling instructions
Missed deadlines

Productivity
Jobs take longer
Erratic/declining productivity
Wide swings in productivity

Assignment Changes
Requests for work with minimal supervision
Requests for work with other suspected substance abusers
Refusal of others to work with suspected abuser

Mood Changes
Unusual flare-ups or temper outbursts
Personality changes
Changes in overall attitude
Overreaction to criticism
Blaming others for mistakes
Wide mood swings

Miscellaneous Signs
Secretive behavior
Numerous suspicious telephone calls or messages
Frequent trips to rest room, locker, or other places away
    from work site

Unreasonable or unexplained financial difficulties
Unreasonable or unexplained wealth
Constant sleepy appearance
Drug paraphernalia at work site
Dramatic change in number or type of friends

Relationships

Difficulties with coworkers
Withdrawal from family
Loner behavior
Disruptive behavior
Overly critical of others
Association with known substance abusers

Injuries and Accidents

More frequent illnesses
Longer recovery from minor illnesses or accidents
Failure to use required safety equipment
Increase in workers' compensation claims

Appearance

Deterioration of overall health, hygiene, and habits
Rapid or extreme weight loss
Major changes in style of dress
Inappropriate wearing of sunglasses
Unusual effort to hide arms with clothes or tattoos

Drug Symptoms

Cocaine

Possible effects: Nasal redness, runny nose, talkativeness, increased alertness, euphoria, loss of appetite, anxiety
Generic names: cocaine, hydrochloride
Street names: coke, snow, uptown, toot, crack, rock
Duration of effects: onset 15–30 seconds; peaks 5–15 minutes; loaded 15–20 minutes; normal 50–90 minutes
Method: oral, injection, smoking, inhalation
Overdose symptoms: agitation, extremely high body temperature, hallucinations, possible death

Noncocaine Stimulants

Possible effects: restlessness, talkativeness, excitation, dry mouth, body tremors, increased alertness, euphoria, insomnia, loss of appetite, anxiety

Trade and generic names: Benzedrine, Biphetamine, Besoxyn, Dexedrine, Metheorine, Preludin, Ritalin, caffeine

Street names: bennies, copilots, black beauties, dex, speed, meth, crank, uppers, beans

Duration: onset: 30–40 minutes; loaded 4–8 hours

Method: oral, injection, smoking, inhalation

Overdose symptoms: agitation, extremely high body temperature, hallucinations, possible death

Phencyclidine

Possible effects: blank stare, cyclic behavior, warm to the touch, perspiring, muscle rigidity, disorientation, repetitive speech, incomplete verbal responses, speech difficulty, noncommunicative, confusion, agitation, increased pain threshold, illusions, combative behavior

Trade and generic names: Ketamine, hydrochloride, Ketalar, Ketaject, Sernyl, Sernylan

Street names: angel dust, crystal, DOA, dust, green, sherms, supercools, WAC, zombie, tictac

Duration of effect: onset 1–5 minutes; peak 15–30 minutes; loaded 4–6 hours; normal 24–48 hours

Method: oral, smoking, injection, eye drops, inhalation

Overdose symptoms: longer and more intense "trips," psychosis, possible death

Hallucinogens

Possible effects: dazed appearance, body tremors, hallucinations, perspiration, memory loss, poor perception of time and distance, lack of coordination, paranoia, muscle tension, hypersensitivity, nausea, disorientation, speech difficulty, flashbacks

Trade and generic names: mescaline, LSD, MDA, peyote, psilocybin

Street names: acid, love drug, cactus, buttons, magic mushrooms, barrels

Duration of effects: variable
Method: oral, smoking, injection, insufflation
Overdose symptoms: severe sweating, high blood pressure, exhibition of very bizarre behaviors, very long "trips," and delusional behavior.

Cannabis

Possible effects: reddening of the eyes, body tremors, marijuana debris in the mouth, odor of burnt marijuana, relaxed inhibitions, disorientation, increased appetite, impaired perception of time and distance, lack of attention, possible paranoia
Generic names: hash oil, hashish, marijuana
Street names: kif, herb, honey, joint, grass, mota, canja, weed, reefer
Duration of effects: onset 8–9 seconds; peak 10–30 minutes; loaded 2–3 hours; normal, variable
Method: smoking, oral
Overdose symptoms: fatigue, paranoia, possible psychosis

Inhalants

Possible effects: odor of substance, possible substance on hands or face, confusion, disorientation, slurred speech, bloodshot, watery, or inflamed eyes
Generic names: amyl nitrite, butyl hirate, toluene, paint thinner, gasoline, nitrous oxide
Street names: glue, locker room, rush, laughing gas, poppers, snappers, kick
Duration of effect: variable
Method: inhalation
Overdose symptoms: coma, possible death

Depressants

Possible effects: drowsiness, lack of coordination, sluggishness, slurred speech, disorientation, drunken behavior
Trade and generic names: Amyial, Dalmane, Doriden, Librium, Seconol, Valium, alcohol, Xanax
Street names: blues, downers, yellow jackets, rainbows, ludes, 714s, booze, reds

Duration of effects: barbiturate 1–16 hours; methaqualone
   4–8 hours; tranquilizer 4–8 hours; chloral hydrate 5–8
   hours
Method: oral, injection
Overdose symptoms: shallow breathing; cold, clammy skin;
   rapid, weak pulse; coma; possible death

Narcotic
Possible effects: droopy eyelids, drowsiness, extremely
   relaxed body composure, depressed reflexes, low raspy
   speech, dry mouth, facial itching, euphoria, fresh
   puncture marks
Trade and generic names: codeine, Demerol, Dilaudid,
   morphine, opium, methadone, Percodan, heroin
Street names: schoolboy, smack, junk, downtown
Duration of effects: for most narcotics, 4–6 hours
Method: oral, injection, inhalation
Overdose symptoms: shallow breathing; cold, clammy skin;
   rapid, weak pulse; coma; possible death

and management staff. The written policy should be clearly displayed and communicated to all employees when hired and at least annually thereafter.

In March 1995, I interviewed Arlin Ciechanowski, a drug recognition expert (DRE), to gain a law enforcement perspective on drug abuse. Ciechanowski has spent most of his career trying to win the war against drugs. He obtained his master's degree in Criminal Justice Administration and received extensive training through the Federal Bureau of Investigation in the area of drug detection and abuse. He now spends his days training other law enforcement officers on how to stay alive while doing their jobs. Part of Ciechanowski's training took him to the streets of Los Angeles, where knowing how to spot illicit drug use sometimes means the difference between going home and going to the morgue.

Ciechanowski is quick to point out that the people he deals with as a street cop are typically not the same ones a supervisor or manager deals with on the job. Many of his cases involve people whose addictions have already made it impossible for them to maintain any type of responsible or stable employment.

Most addicts, Ciechanowski says, were at one time in the work force before drugs became the ruling force in their lives. Eventually, poor performance and absenteeism as a result of drug or alcohol abuse cost them their jobs. Education is a useful tool for managers and supervisors to help them detect alcohol and drug abuse in the workplace. With training and assistance programs, there might be a chance to rehabilitate employees and help them straighten out their lives.

When asked why drug abuse is so prevalent in today's society, Ciechanowski says that for kids in many cities, it is easier to be involved in drugs than not be involved in drugs. "A fourteen-year-old can make five thousand dollars a week selling cocaine," he says. "Cocaine is more expensive than gold when compared ounce to ounce. With availability of money like that, there's a powerful motivation for kids to sell drugs."

Employers today must be concerned about drug abuse among juveniles because these kids will enter the work force when they are older. Not only are kids becoming involved with hard-core drugs, but they're experimenting with all sorts of other dangerous, and potentially fatal, drugs.

Ciechanowski points out that it isn't just young people doing drugs. "Sixty million prescriptions for tranquilizers are written during a typical year," he says. "While many of the people taking these tranquilizers are doing so legally, they are definitely showing up at their workstations with their ability to perform their jobs being severely impaired. Add to that the 20 percent of males, ages twenty-five to thirty-four, who use marijuana at least once per month, and companies are facing a labor force that is making decisions based on impaired capabilities."

The first thing supervisors need to do if they suspect an employee may be under the influence of drugs or alcohol is to remove the employee from areas that could be unsafe. The employee should not be allowed to operate a motor vehicle or any heavy equipment. Do not leave suspected abusers unattended; if their abilities are diminished, they may act in a manner that is dangerous to themselves.

When a drug overdose is suspected, emergency medical attention should be sought for the employee. Even if the employee will refuse treatment from paramedics, an ambulance should still be called. Remember, the employee's decision-making skills may be impaired as a result of the substance abuse.

Two or more people should be assigned to watch the employee. Some drugs, such as angel dust and PCP, could compel the employee to have delusions and become combative. A person under the influence of PCP could fight a dozen people under the mistaken belief that he or she is in a life-or-death struggle. Some people become assaultive when under the influence of alcohol. At the first sign of combative behavior, call law enforcement officials. Certain drugs produce violent behaviors, and because of the impairment and the effects of the drugs, the user will feel no pain at all. The lack of response to pain makes restraining the individual impossible.

The two people watching the employee should document all of their observations regarding the employee. Having two similar reports of the incident provides a stronger justification for intervention. When documenting the behavior and the actions of the employee with drug- or alcohol-impaired abilities, record the company policy that is affected by the performance. For example, if the employee failed to wear required personal protection equipment such as safety goggles because he refused to take off his sunglasses, then the documentation should reflect not only the actions of the employee, but also the violation of the company policy regarding safety equipment.

Witnesses should document their observations regarding the employee's behavior. Statements made by the employee and the time, date, action, and location all need to be included in the report. The actions taken by management in response to the situation should also be recorded. If law enforcement officials are called in to respond to the situation, they should be asked to provide management with a copy of their report. Each of these reports should be placed in the employee's personnel file. Later, if a lawsuit is brought against the company, the documentation will help defend the company's actions.

The supervisor should not attempt to counsel or discipline an impaired employee. The supervisor should also refrain from making moral judgments. An intoxicated employee is not in a frame of mind to comprehend the gravity of the situation. Give him or her time to recover from the effects of the substance. The confrontation can take place later.

When you do confront the employee, you should have written documentation of the incidents and the breaches in company policy. Prepare in advance an action plan for the employee's improvement along with specific performance objectives. Supply, in writing, to the employee time frames for completing the performance objectives.

Do not to try to diagnose or treat the employee's problem. The majority of supervisors do not have the training to deal with alcohol or drug problems. Instead, refer the individual to an employee-assistance program or to a counseling agency staffed with professionals trained in substance abuse. More information on counseling problem employees is provided in Chapter 6.

DOMESTIC VIOLENCE IN THE WORKPLACE

Domestic violence is an issue that every business should address. It is present everywhere, whether the signs of it are recognized or not. The damages caused by domestic violence can have a significant impact on a company's bottom line. The Bureau of National Affairs estimates that companies lose $3 to $5 billion each year as a result of domestic violence.[8] According to the 1993 Census of Fatal Occupational Injuries, 4 percent of work-related homicides stem from personal relationships.[9]

The job performance of employees who become involved in abusive relationships is negatively affected. Absenteeism, stress, and medical problems increase. Each of these problems carries its own sizable price tag. The increased potential for internal acts of violence cannot be ignored either.

Statistics vary on the extent of domestic abuse in the United States. The American Medical Association estimates that almost four million women are victims of severe assaults by boyfriends and husbands each year. One woman in four is likely to be abused by a partner at some time in her life.[10]

According to another source, "even the minimum estimates indicate that at least 2 million women in the United States are severely assaulted (e.g., on an aggravated assault level) by a male partner during an average 12 month period. Researchers in the field agree that a more accurate national estimate would be a figure of 4 million women severely assaulted by male partners annually, and an estimate of 40 percent of adult couples having experienced at least one aggressive incident in their current relationship."[11] Men also are the victims of assault by both other men and women. While this text focuses on female victims, this information is also pertinent to men involved in abusive relationships. This type of threat cannot be ignored.

Any police officer will tell you that a domestic dispute is one of the most dangerous and difficult calls to handle. The parties are typically very agitated and angry. To add further obstacles, often one or both people are highly intoxicated, and their behavior is unpredictable. When police offers attempt to intervene, the parties can easily turn on them. If you accept the statistic of a 25 percent abuse rate, apply that figure to the number of employees in your business. It almost seems inconceivable that 25 out of every 100 employees has been, or is currently involved in, an abusive relationship.

The sad truth is that most people, at some time in their lives, experience a bad or failed relationship with a domestic partner, spouse, or lover. These failed relationships often involve many more people than the two who are facing the difficulties. Children, parents, in-laws, neighbors, and friends also commonly get involved in the ending of a relationship. Often, other employees who are friends with the separating couple get absorbed into the relationship.

As a coworker, boss, or business owner, we have many reasons to want to assist the abused employee. She might be somebody we have worked side by side with for years. We might care deeply about this person's well-being. We don't want anything bad to happen to her. We hate to see her face the pain of an abusive relationship. The bruises that she disguises make us fear that the worst will happen the next time supper is late or she forgets to take out the garbage. Person to person, we care.

As an employer, we have several reasons to be concerned. We care for the abused employee as a person and detest seeing her in physical and emotional pain. We also have a significant amount of time and resources invested in the employee's training and education. A considerable amount of money has been invested to screen, hire, and place the employee. Replacing her with a new employee would be a costly proposition.

Managers are also concerned about the costs of the employee's decreased productivity. How can anybody give 110 percent to a job when his or her personal life is in a state of turmoil? It is unreasonable to take an employee who has not slept in days, is worried about feeding the children, or has bill collectors calling, situate her in the front office, and expect her to be Mary Poppins.

Supervisors and managers should pay attention to the warning signs of domestic abuse. This may seem like meddling into an employee's personal life, and it may make you uncomfortable. Turn the situation around, and focus on the lost efficiency of the employee. View the situation as a managerial problem that must be resolved.

Abused employees frequently have evidence of bruises or broken bones. They may try to hide the bruises with makeup or wear long-sleeved shirts and pants. They may say they had an accident at home. Be suspicious when an employee professes to have experienced numerous accidents. People generally do not fall down the same set of steps on a weekly basis, and they learn not to walk into walls after a couple of mishaps. Absenteeism and tardiness may increase due to the employee's doctor appointments. Seldom do these situations improve without intervention.

The abused employee may be suffering from depression, which could be signified by frequent crying or other observable symptoms. The employee might talk about suicide. A significant weight gain or loss may be readily observed.

As a supervisor or manager, you can be a resource for the abused employee. Remember, though, that you are neither a marital counselor nor a psychologist, and you should not pretend to be. Do not tell the employee what to do, and do not pretend to know what she is going through. As a leader, you can help the employee in a variety of other ways.

Be empathetic to the employee's problems, and try to understand what the employee is going through and how she feels. Give the employee the opportunity to talk as much as she is willing to. Often, out of embarrassment or humiliation, abused employees are unwilling to give too many details of either the problems they face at home or the abuse that they are facing. Listen to the employee talk; allow her to cry. You may be the only resource she has. Many times, abused women need somebody, anybody, to listen to them and to show them support.

In many cases of marital abuse, the victim experiences a major lack of self-esteem. Allowing her to talk and offering empathy may make her feel much stronger than she felt before. It certain cases, the employee may feel a tremendous amount of relief by being able to expose the abuse to an empathetic ear.

Refer the victim of domestic abuse to an employee-assistance program (EAP) if one is available. If an EAP is not available, refer the employee to a community resource for battered spouses. Offer to stay in the room while the employee makes the initial call to either the EAP agency or the community resource. If the employee does not want you in the room, she will probably tell you so. If she does ask you to leave the room while she makes the initial call, tell her either that you will wait outside the room or that you will be back in ten or fifteen minutes. The circumstances will dictate the best route to take. Gentle prodding to pick up the telephone may be what the employee needs to start a recovery program. Do not try to force an employee to take actions that she doesn't want to take. You cannot make the status of an employee's personal life a condition of employment if the employee's job performance is otherwise acceptable. You can, however, make the satisfactory performance of job-related duties a condition of employment.

Do not expect a miracle overnight just because the victim of domestic abuse does make the initial call. The employee is involved in a difficult situation, and there are no easy answers. It often takes years for the actual problem to develop, and it cannot be solved overnight. There are certain employees who will not be helped no matter what you do for them. Be prepared to face and accept this. After everything you do to help the employee, you must realize that the abused employee is the chief player in this problem and that she must make her own decisions. After all, she has to live with them.

In a worst-case scenario, the abuser may show up at the workplace. When this happens, the threat of violence enlarges to include all employees, customers, and visitors at the workplace. Most security professionals have dealt with this type of problem before.

In a typical situation, the estranged husband shows up at nine o'clock in the morning, stone drunk. He has spent the last two hours in a local tavern, building his confidence and determining to set his wife straight. He shows up on the company doorstep with his own personal motive in mind and no regard for security policy and procedure. The wife is usually highly embarrassed as her husband is escorted from the premises by security officers.

That situation is mild compared with the other accounts we read in the daily papers. For example, on January 7, 1995, a forty-three-year-old man allegedly walked into the Ford Motor plant in Plymouth Township, Michigan, with a gun. According to reports, he opened fire on his thirty-nine-year-old estranged wife, shooting her in the legs and the abdomen. As a friend came to her aid, he was mortally shot. Witnesses report that the man then turned the gun on himself. Both the wife and her coworker died shortly after the incident. This type of scenario is repeated all too often across the United States.

According to the U.S. Department of Labor, in 1992 one-sixth of the incidents of violence against women in the workplace were committed by a present or former spouse or boyfriend.[12] In many instances, the workplace is the only place where the assailant is sure to find the employee.

STALKING

Even though stalking is a relatively new topic in the security field, it has existed for many years. Most experienced security professionals have been involved in an incident in which an employee was being stalked by another person, often the employee's estranged spouse.

In Schuyler, Nebraska, history repeated itself on March 3, 1995, when, for the second time since 1989, two employees were shot and killed in the parking lot of the Excel Corporation. In the latest incident, a man shot his common-law wife and the man with whom she had been living. Both victims died instantly after being shot in the head. The gunman then committed suicide. In November 1989, a man had shot and killed his wife and her male companion in the same parking lot as they arrived for work. He was arrested and convicted of the murders and is now serving two consecutive life sentences.

Only recently have laws specifically related to stalking been passed. In 1990, California became the first state to pass antistalking legislation. Since then, almost all of the other states have followed suit and adopted similar legislation. The federal government has also enacted laws that protect women from violence. The Violence Against Women Act was passed into law in March 1995 as part of the Crime Bill. The bill established the first Violence Against Women Office at the Department of Justice.

The language used in California's antistalking law was adopted by other states. In California, two major components are necessary for the stalking law to be applicable. First, a repeated pattern of harassment must be present. Following a person satisfies this component. The key word in the first component is *repeated.* Some states define *repeated* as simply more than once; other states have criteria that require two incidents within twenty-four hours. Second, the element of threat against the person must be present. Laws differ from state to state as to the level of threat required. In some states, the victim only needs to feel threatened; elsewhere, additional measures are required to determine the level of threat involved.

By 1993, forty-seven states had adopted antistalking laws. For more information on the stalking laws applicable in your state, call your local law enforcement agency.

The workplace is the prime target for stalkers to pursue their victims. Victims can change their home telephone number, change the vehicle they drive, and even move to a new house or apartment. One thing they usually cannot do easily is change jobs. The victims still go to the same place of business on the same days and at the same times. Chances are they still have the same lunch and break schedule and still park in the same spot. The stalkers, especially when estranged spouses, know the habits of their victim.

The victim of a stalking may find notes on the car, receive unwanted flowers and numerous telephone calls, and suffer a host of other nuisances. Stalkers usually follow their victims constantly and know where they are at all times.

Victims are often not willing to let company security officials know that they are being stalked until the situation becomes dangerous. They may be reluctant to talk to a stranger about this very personal subject. Victims of stalking may live in quiet desperation, not knowing where to turn and not wanting others to know their fears and anxieties. In some circumstances, they may not call the police for fear of enraging the stalker. When the victim is fearful of the potential actions of the stalker, police assistance can be of little use. When the victim does call the police, they may be unable to help because a crime has not yet been committed. Not all states have laws dealing with stalking. When the police do get involved, it may end up as one person's word against the other's. This is especially true when the two parties have had a previous intimate relationship. Some states have laws regarding these types of cases.

Cases of stalking have continued for years. David Letterman has been stalked by a woman since 1988. She has posed as his wife and broken into his house numerous times. Once when Letterman was out of town, she stole his car and drove it for several days before being caught. Injunctions were of little help in resolving the matter. Between 1988 and 1993, the woman was arrested eight times.

Rebecca Schaeffer, the star of "My Sister Sam," was the stalking victim of an obsessed fan. It all ended tragically on July 19, 1989, when she opened her apartment door and was fatally shot in the chest with a .357 magnum. The stalker was arrested and convicted of her murder. He is now in prison, serving a life sentence without the possibility of parole. The tragedy touched the hearts of the nation as people became painfully aware of the case through heart-felt statements by Rebecca Schaeffer's family, friends, and coworkers. Costar Pam Dawber faced the cameras and shared her anguish as she mourned the loss of her friend and coworker.

Celebrity stalking cases can get a great deal of attention, but the symptoms of a pursued employee in the company may not be so evident. The employer can be made aware of the stalking in a number of ways. Ideally, the stalking victim should go to the security department for assistance, but this isn't always the case. A friend or coworker may talk to security officers about the situation out of fear for the victim's safety or their own. The supervisor or manager may become aware of the situation after observing a decrease in productivity or performance. Security officers may discover the truth after incidents in the parking lot. The receptionist may suspect the problem when the employee repeatedly refuses telephone calls, flowers, or other deliveries from a particular individual. The security or the human resource department may become aware that a problem exists after other employees report suspicious activities involving the stalker or the victim. Employees who report this type of problem should be allowed to remain anonymous.

Another type of stalking case involves employees (current or former) who stalk supervisory or managerial personnel. The supervisor who fires or disciplines an employee may become the center of the employee's frustrations. The employee may feel that the action taken by management was personally motivated and may, as a result, begin a campaign to destroy the supervisor's life. The crusade may include such typical stalking actions as repeated threats, telephone calls, following the victim, or sitting outside the person's home or office.

Romantic obsessions, or erotomania, take place when one employee is the recipient of the unwanted affections of another person. The stalker develops an obsession with the victim and believes that fate has bound them together. The employee on the receiving end of this obsession often experiences an overwhelming display of the other person's fixation. If the stalking victim is involved with another person, that person is often the target of death threats. Because this other person stands in the way of the stalker's desire to become involved with the victim, the stalker believes that by taking the third party out of the picture, he or she will succeed with the fascination.

Once the company becomes aware that a problem exists, it faces a dilemma: What actions should be taken to protect not only the targeted employee, but all employees? Businesses in general seem to frown on getting too involved in their employees' personal problems, even with just cause for concern. Just referring the employee to an EAP offers very little protection for the company or the employee. A more aggressive action plan is often called for in this type of situation. Emotional support is beneficial, but not a cure-all, for the employee in this situation. Larger cities may have support groups available for victims. A support group may provide emotional support to the employee as well as offer practical advice on ways for victims to protect themselves. The other members may have encountered, or are still encountering, the same feelings and experiences. (See the box "Tips for Victims of Stalking.")

In many ways, the profile of the stalker mirrors that of the potentially violent person (discussed in the next chapter). Al-

Tips for Victims of Stalking

1. Document every contact with the stalker. This includes all telephone calls, messages, letters, and deliveries and all cases of being followed or watched. The documentation will help you prove you are being stalked.
2. Contact the police department every time the stalker makes any kind of contact. The police department should also maintain documentation. Ask for copies of the police reports.
3. Use an answering machine or a caller-identification service to screen calls. Have a trace put on your telephone and change to an unlisted number. Give the new telephone number only to people with a need to know. Consider using a pager to screen emergency calls. A mobile telephone can provide access to emergency services when you are in your car or away from the telephone.
4. Advise your friends, neighbors, coworkers, and family members of the situation. Have neighbors watch for any unusual activities on or near your home.
5. Keep the outside of your home well lit and free of excessive bushes or trees that might provide a stalker with a place to hide.
6. Install extra locks, lights, and door alarms. Consider getting a large dog.
7. Join a support group, or seek other outside support. Get assistance from other local agencies.
8. File an injunction against the stalker. Talk to an attorney about other legal tactics.
9. Never enter into conversation with the stalker. Most stalkers are very persuasive and are able to solicit a response (typically an angry one) from the victim.
10. Consider enrolling in a self-defense class. Pepper spray and mace are good self-defense tools. Don't automatically buy a gun. Weapons are very dangerous to have around and often lead to other problems.
11. Keep another person with you as much as possible when running errands.

though the majority of cases involve men stalking women, women also stalk men, as in the case of David Letterman.

REFERENCES

1. "SHRM Reveals Extent of Workplace Violence," *EAP Digest* (March–April 1994): 25.

2. CAL/OSHA Guidelines for Workplace Security (Department of Industrial Relations, Division of Occupational Safety and Health, San Francisco, August 15, 1994), p. 4.

3. Ibid., p. 6.

4. Alcohol, Drug Abuse, and Mental Health Administration, U.S. Department of Health and Human Services, *The Economic Costs of Alcohol and Drug Abuse and Mental Illness: 1985* (Washington, D.C.: U.S. Government Printing Office, 1990).

5. L.D. Johnson, P.M. O'Malley, and J.G. Bachman, *National Survey Results on Drug Use from the Monitoring the Future Survey, 1975–1993* (Washington, D.C.: U.S. Department of Health and Human Services, 1994), pp. 6–9.

6. "Why the Violence? Workers Respond," *EAP Digest* (March–April 1994): 10.

7. F.J. Dickman, W.G. Emener, and W.S. Hutchison, Jr., *Counseling the Troubled Person in Industry* (Springfield, IL: Thomas Publications, 1985), p. 23.

8. Lisa Genasci, "More Companies See Domestic Violence as a Workplace Issue," *Waterloo Courier*, 25 December 1994, p. B1.

9. U.S. Department of Labor, Bureau of Labor Statistics, *News*, 10 August 1994, p. 3.

10. S. Glazer, "Violence against Women," *CQ Researcher* 3 (February 1993): 171.

11. *Statistics Package*, 3rd ed. (Philadelphia: National Clearinghouse for the Defense of Battered Women, February 1994), p. 91.

12. J. Windau and G. Toscano, *Workplace Homicides in 1992* (Washington, D.C.: U.S. Department of Labor, Bureau of Labor Statistics, February 1994), p. 2.

3

The Violent Person

PROFILE OF THE VIOLENT PERSON

Establishing profiles of the disgruntled employee who may return to work in a violent manner is a dangerous proposition. Stereotyping employees into narrowly defined classifications could establish a propensity to look for employees who fit into the profiles and ignore threats or intimidations made by others. There is not one certain genetic makeup of the violent employee. Employee violence is committed by a spectrum of people under a variety of circumstances.

However, based on the case histories of workplace violence, researchers have developed a profile into which a significant portion of the offenders fit. Most offenders are white males between the ages of twenty-five and forty-five. They have been employed with the same company for a long period of time (that is, they are typically not new or temporary employees), and they often have strong personal ties with their job.

This profile has limited value to the employer. Profiles do not serve as predictors of future violence. They only serve to describe workers who have in the past returned violently to the workplace. Behaviors and warning signs should be used to evaluating the level of danger that might exist. When determining the mental condition of an employee, the first thing that you must look at is the individual's behavior. As with counseling and coaching meetings, the focus of an employee-assistance program must be the behavior of the employee and not his or her physical characteristics. Behavior is the key to intervention and prevention of violence. (See the box "Assessing the Violent Person.")

WARNING SIGNS OF VIOLENT BEHAVIOR

You can help protect your company from acts of aggression by learning to identify the signs that precede violence by employees, customers, or visitors and by following the recommended guidelines. Once you've learned to recognize these signs, you must respond in an appropriate manner to the perceived level of the threat. If the warning signs indicate an immediate danger, immediately notify the local police or sheriff's department. If the indications point to future acts of aggression, alert the company's human resources and security departments. The intervention plan must meet the degree of threat anticipated.

There is no single all-inclusive list of predictable behaviors that a violent person will exhibit. There are, however, common indicators that mark a person's disposition to engage in violent acts. (See the box "Warning Signs of Violent Behavior.") Caution must be exercised in interpreting these warning signs. One warning sign, if significant, may be all that's needed to determine that additional evaluation is required. However, victims of violent acts by a coworker usually agree that more than one warning sign was present.

In at least one situation, this was not the case. John Taylor had always been considered a model employee at the Orange Glen Post Office in California. Taylor had received numerous awards for

---

Assessing the Violent Person

- Do not depend on profiles to predict violent behavior.
- There is no all-inclusive list of predictable behaviors for violent individuals.
- Model employees have produced violent behavior.
- You must evaluate an employee's behavior to determine his or her propensity for violence.
- People who are known to have exhibited a history of violence in the past may have a tendency for violence in the future.
- Claims of the exotic or strange may indicate that an employee is losing touch with reality.
- Alcohol and drug abuse are common among people who have committed violence in the workplace.
- After incidents of workplace violence, many people say that the disgruntled employee had a fascination with weapons.
- Employees who say, "What happened there could happen here," may be issuing a warning of their own future actions.

---

his good job performance. He was well liked and enjoyed sociable relationships with friends and coworkers. Underneath his model behavior, however, something must have been very wrong. On August 10, 1989, Taylor shot and killed his wife in their home before he went to work. He brought one hundred rounds of ammunition and a .22 caliber semiautomatic weapon with him that day. He killed two coworkers and injured others before killing himself. Even after the rampage, most coworkers felt that he had always been an exemplary employee. They were left struggling to determine what could have gone so wrong in Taylor's life that he felt that this was his only solution.

Warning Signs of Violent Behavior

- Threats of physical violence or statements about getting even
- History of violence against coworkers, family members, other people, or animals
- History of failed relationships with family members, spouses, friends, or coworkers
- Lack of a social support system (i.e., friends and family)
- Paranoia and distrust of others
- Blaming others for life's failures and problems
- Claims of strange events, such as visits from UFOs
- Alcohol or drug abuse on or off the job
- Frequent tardiness and absenteeism
- Concentration, performance, or safety-related problems
- Carrying or concealing a weapon at work (security officers, police officers, etc. excepted)
- Obsession with weapons, often exotic weapons
- Fascination with stories of violence, especially those that happen at a workplace, such as frequent discussions of the post office slayings
- History of intimidation against other people
- High levels of frustration, easily angered
- Diminished self-esteem
- Inability to handle stressful situations
- Romantic obsession with a coworker

Threats

Employees who make comments about getting even with managers, supervisors, or other employees for disciplinary actions or dismissal should be taken seriously. The followup to these threats can range from flattening car tires to murder. The degree of threat depends on what is said and the manner in which it is said.

Almost everybody in the security and human resources professions has heard a seemingly simple comment that made the hair on the back of their neck stand on end. Without the need for additional words, the insinuation was clear. The manner of what is said and the appropriateness of the remark are clues to possible future actions. When in doubt, report the conversation to others who can assist you—perhaps the human resources or security department. If you are a member of either of those departments, don't hesitate to make the conversation known to others on your team. The threats may be idle, or they may not. Until the intent is known, caution must be exercised.

Ignored threats can lead to tragedy. In Royal Oak, Michigan, a thirty-one-year-old postal worker, Thomas McIlvane, told many people of his intentions to kill his coworkers. He also made threats by telephone. On November 14, 1991, McIlvane followed through with his threats. Before turning the gun on himself, he engaged in a shooting rampage that left three of his coworkers dead and six others wounded. McIlvane died two days later from his self-inflicted injuries.

History of Violence

People who are known to have committed acts of violence against family members, fellow employees, acquaintances, or animals should be considered as having a propensity toward violence. They have already exhibited behaviors that show a lack of respect for others. This is one of the reasons why background checks on applicants for employment are vital to the well-being of any business. People typically act as they have acted before, and history has a way of repeating itself. If a potential employee has a history of assaults or threats, the company may be best suited in the long run to keep looking for other candidates. (More is covered on this topic in Chapter 6.)

History of Failed Relationships

Employees who are known to have a history of failed relationships with spouses, family members, or friends may lack the support network that many people naturally take for granted. Employees who have no resources for venting their concerns and frustrations with others who have a genuine concern for their well-being may be a potential problem. Employee-assistance programs can provide some support for these people and should not be overlooked as a resource. Employees who commit violence in the workplace often do not have family and friends in whom they feel they can confide.

Potentially volatile employees may also have a history of interpersonal conflicts with coworkers, especially supervisory and management personnel. They may be unable to maintain good relationships with others for any period of time, or they may abandon relationships with other employees. They may isolate themselves from society. They often sit alone on breaks and during lunch due to their inability to develop relationships with coworkers.

Distrust and Suspicion

An employee's failure to get along with others, especially supervisors and managers, can lead to distrust and suspicion. Potentially violent employees may have a severe distrust of others. They may blame others for their problems and may refuse to accept any level of personal responsibility. They may believe that everybody is out to get them. Increased errors might be blamed on other employees' purposely sabotaging their work. They may claim that the manager or supervisor is planning on terminating their employment for a variety of reasons. In many of these situations, the employer may not be contemplating any action against the employee.

When the supervisor does try to counsel potentially violent employees to improve their job performance or behavior, they may refuse to accept any type of coaching and take all statements as personal criticism. Long-lasting grudges develop. To employees like this, the supervisor or manager may become the nucleus of their perceived injustice and all of their personal and professional problems. This nucleus can expand to include human resources professionals, union representatives, or others whom the employee feels are part of the conspiracy. Many employees who return to the workplace to kill their coworkers are target driven. Their supervisors, managers, human resources professionals, or union representatives are often on the list of victims.

This was the case when Paul Hannah, a lineman for the telephone company in Chicago, was suspended for refusing to take a drug test. He shot at the company manager, but the gun misfired six times. The gun eventually fired properly, and the union steward who tried to intervene was killed.

In times when layoffs are pending and everybody in the company feels a lack of job security, emotionally distressed employees will have exaggerated feelings of paranoia and distrust. Because they are often on the targeted layoff list due to poor performance, they may sabotage other employees' work to make their performance look better. When they do receive their pink slip or demotion due to the downsizing, they feel that their suspicions were proven, regardless of the underlying reasons. They may share feelings of "I told you so, but nobody would listen." If the company's management does not recognize the threat, the unstable employee could go unnoticed until he shows up at the receptionist's desk one day with a gun. This obviously means too little attention to the threat, too late. There are no winners.

This was the case in Tampa, Florida, in 1992 when Paul Calden returned to his former workplace, Fireman's Insurance Company. When he had been fired eight months earlier, he had told employees, "You ain't seen the last of me." When Calden returned, he shot the human resources manager, saying, "This is what you get for firing me." In total, three men died and two women were injured. Calden later killed himself.

Unusual Claims

Claims of the exotic and strange could be an indication that an employee is losing contact with reality and suffering from mental illness. When employees claim to have had personal visits from aliens, the president of the United States, or Jesus Christ, there is reason for concern. Referral to an employee-assistance program or intervention plan should be implemented.

Alcohol or Drug Abuse

Alcohol or drug abuse is a common malady of people who commit acts of violence in the workplace as current or former employees, customers, or others. Alcohol and drugs can lower inhibitions and grant a false sense of security. Financial problems may be the motivation for the criminal act in cases such as robbery. The offender needs money to support a habit, and other methods of obtaining money may not be available.

Employees facing drug and alcohol problems can be referred to an employee assistance program for help. When job-related performance problems like absenteeism and tardiness are a result of substance abuse, the employee should be referred. As a supervisor, you cannot make an employee accept help for an addiction, but you can make it known that future employment depends on improved job performance.

Ownership of Weapons

Employees who are known to own weapons or belong to clubs in which weapons are the major focus should be considered capable of procuring weapons that might later be used against other employees. In the majority of cases, however, owning a gun is not illegal. In the United States, bearing arms is a constitutional right—a right that many citizens actively exercise. Major organizations, such as the National Rifle Association (NRA), provide lobbying support in the crusade to retain the right to own weapons. Millions of Americans own guns for self-protection, hunting, sportsmanship, investment, or other personal reasons. Most people who own weapons do not do so to commit criminal acts against others. Ownership of weapons is a personal choice for everybody, except minors and convicted felons. Much like abortion, gambling, and religion, the right to bear arms is a topic that reeks of politics and emotion.

Mandatory waiting periods for weapon-purchase permits are typically referred to as *cooling-off periods*. People who want to purchase a weapon as a means to express an irrational and often violent action will have the opportunity and the time to calm themselves down and take care of whatever problem they may be trying to resolve in a more productive manner. The cooling-off period also allows the issuing agency time to investigate the applicant's background for prior criminal convictions or a history of mental instability.

Employees who keep loaded weapons at home or in their vehicles have almost immediate access to them, and hence the calming-down period is not available. Never assume that an employee has a license to carry a gun. Even when the employee does display a license, you can still ban the weapon from company-owned property. Weapons are not appropriate in the work environment. Employees who threaten to use a weapon against others are an immediate concern, whether they have a weapon in their possession or not.

Anytime you discover that an employee has carried a weapon into the workplace, you must take immediate action. Notify the local police to assist in the intervention. Managers, supervisors, and human resource people should not take on the task of confronting an armed employee alone. You may be asked to assist the police department in determining the level of immediate danger present.

It could be that an employee with a shotgun in his truck forgot to put it away when he returned from a hunting trip. In this situation, the employee will most likely understand that the intervention is necessary to ensure the safety and security of the other employees. On the other hand, an employee with a history of threats and intimidation may not appreciate the police showing up to remove the weapon, but at that point, who cares? Threats in the workplace create a climate of fear that can affect employees as dramatically as actual violence. Employees who are afraid may not show up for work, and those who do will not be productive.[1]

Your company has a legal obligation to provide a safe and secure work environment free from all recognized hazards. Obviously, a disgruntled employee with a weapon is a big hazard, and you must exercise extreme caution. Employee safety is the primary concern; protecting the company from civil lawsuits is secondary.

Fascination with Weapons

Disgruntled employees who have committed violence against co-workers often owned or talked about highly exotic weapons. This fascination frequently includes a passion for weapons that are not typically associated with self-defense, hunting, or common gun collecting. Potentially violent employees may own a large number of exotic weapons, such as automatic rifles with elaborate scopes, AK47s, swords, bayonets, and the like.

Fascination with Workplace Violence

Another indicator that an employee may use violence or intimidation to rectify a perceived injustice, or in some cases a real injustice, is the employee's fixation on incidents of workplace violence. The employee may talk a lot about post office slayings or other cases where a worker used violence.

It is common for employees to discuss incidents of violence that have occurred in their city or at an affiliated business. Some of this talk is productive, as it enables employees to discuss their feelings with others in a supportive environment. After acts of workplace violence, it can be therapeutic and aid in the healing process when employees share their feelings with their coworkers.

However, employees who say things like, "What happened there could happen here," may be issuing a warning of their own actions. When this type of statement is made in conjunction with other warning signs, a serious situation is developing and an intervention plan needs to be implemented.

History of Harassment or Intimidation

When employees harass and intimidate their coworkers, you must deal with them in a swift and impartial fashion. A no-tolerance corporate policy must be enforced for the benefit of all employees.

When you fail to deal with intimidation, you send a signal that the company condones this type of behavior. Productivity will suffer, and the organization could lose valuable long-term employees who choose to work in a less hostile environment.

In summary, employees who do not fit the typical mold, feel they are persecuted by others, have little or no natural support group, talk extensively about exotic events, including politics, religion, and visits from unlikely people, and are known to have ready access to firearms may be your biggest threat. Take them seriously. To ignore an employee who is threatening and intimidating people at work is to encourage more of the same.[2]

REFERENCES

1. B. Filipczak, "Armed and Dangerous at Work," *Training* (July 1993): 41.
2. Ibid., 41.

II

Before Workplace Violence Occurs

4

Employment Conditions and Violence

INGREDIENTS FOR A VOLATILE WORKPLACE

Violence that erupts at the workplace is like a recipe. When the wrong ingredients are mixed together, a very dangerous, yet predictable, outcome can occur. (See the box "Ingredients for a Volatile Workplace.")

Many managerial books were written during the last twenty-five years. Each one of these claims to tell the "right" way to conduct the business of employing people. Few of these books on the various styles and philosophies of managerial behavior appear today on MBA reading lists. As times are changing, a new management style is emerging, more humane and responsive than in the past. The autocratic management style, in which the supervisor figuratively stands over the employees with a whip, is no longer acceptable. Productivity and employee satisfaction improve when the workplace is an environment of trust and respect. People want to be treated with respect and consideration. When managers and supervisors forget this key element, they create an environment that is ripe for trouble. The experts who have studied workplace killings nearly all agree that many times a contributing factor was a rigid, almost paramilitary work culture.[1]

Ideally, every employee will accept the company's mission statement and adopt its goals on a personal level. The truth is that a lot of employees never do. They see themselves as there to do a job. They could care less about return on equity, strategic business plans, and the like as long as these things don't affect their job security. These employees have a personal agenda: They are just trying to earn a living before going home at the end of the day. They don't want extra hours or extra responsibilities unless the pay makes it worthwhile. This is neither entirely right nor wrong; it's just the way things are.

When these employees exist in a company—and all companies have them—management may try to force them into different departments or try to encourage higher levels of productivity from them. Global competition is forcing every company to get the most out of every resource, including employees. When the competitor's employees are more dedicated and productive than yours, the future of your company may be at stake. Management is under tremendous pressure to produce.

Employees will resent these actions, and problems can easily develop between labor and management. Labor-management disputes are characteristic of work environments that are conducive to employee violence. An upset employee may feel wrongfully charged with acts of workplace misconduct or poor performance. Remember that one of the characteristics of potentially dangerous employees is paranoia—the belief that management is out to get them. Management that responds poorly to the needs of employees can help perpetuate these feelings in the dysfunctional person.

Work environments that produce a multitude of grievances by employees are also indicative of trouble. Management must take a

Ingredients for a Volatile Workplace

- The highly competitive nature of business causes high levels of stress with employees, supervisors, and managers.
- Problems between labor and management can create an "us versus them" atmosphere among some employees.
- Work environments that produce a large number of grievances can be conducive to acts of workplace violence.
- Certain kinds of stress are productive, but a high level of stress can be very destructive and can later foster an environment conducive to violence.
- Rigid, almost paramilitary work cultures foster bitterness and resentment that can lead to violent behavior.

serious look at the types of grievances filed by employees to determine the problems that exist. If the grievances lead to the realization that employees are unhappy with the company's management style, the company needs to take these matters to heart.

What changes can be made to improve employee attitudes? Are the grievances centered around a specific person or department? Are the complaints symptomatic of deep-rooted problems within your company? For now, don't even consider the propensity for violence; just think about the damage to your company's bottom line. Unhappy employees are less productive, and your company risks losing valued employees to other, less distressed, businesses. Employees are the greatest and most valuable asset that your company has. Just as a construction company would not leave its wood out to rot, don't leave employees rotting in bitterness and resentment.

The anger and rage of unhappy employees can be expressed in the form of increased work-related accidents. Workers who are upset and preoccupied with labor problems pay less attention to their jobs. They may feel rushed, or they simply may not care about the job they're doing. They may not pay attention to what is going on around them because they are focusing on the latest rumors and gossip.

An increase in the number of on-the-job accidents means an increase in the number of workers' compensation claims. Employees who believe that the company owes them more than what they are getting may use an accident claim to get what they want: a large settlement, an extended "paid vacation" to recover from their alleged injuries, or attention from their peers. Whatever the cause of on-the-job accidents or the motivations of an employee filing a claim, the increased costs and lost productivity are not in the best interests of the company.

Claims of stress-related disabilities are gaining widespread popularity. In the vast majority of cases, the attending physician or psychiatrist finds the employer responsible for a significant portion of the stress. During an interview, Kenneth Wernimont, a clinical social worker, noted that as many as 30 percent of the patients who seek professional counseling do so as the result of job-induced stressors. In these cases, the company must actively work with the employee and his or her doctor and mental-health provider and the workers' compensation insurance carrier.

When the employee's claim is perfectly valid, you will want to start resolving the problems and get the employee back to work at least part-time. When the claim is less than legitimate, be prepared for the big ride. Stress claims can result in huge disability settlements and enormous paid leaves of absence. Preventing stress claims is less expensive than resolving them later.

There is no denying that stress exists in nearly every workplace throughout the United States. Certain levels of stress are needed to promote a productive and satisfying work environment. Most people operate more efficiently when they are faced with moderate stress. How each person handles stress in important.

Think of the report due in the near future. You will probably keep the deadline for the report in mind as you schedule your other work-related activities. Ideally, you will have time to complete the report in a satisfactory manner and turn it in. Knowing that the report is due keeps you working toward accomplishing that goal. What would happen if the deadline for the report was eliminated or set back a year? Many people would drop the report off their to-do list in a heartbeat and move on to other more pressing things. Without a new deadline, the report may never get done. The stress created by deadlines keeps people focused on getting the job done. Remove the deadlines, hence the stress, and motivation for completing job assignments diminishes and productivity goes down.

Another example of productive stress occurs almost daily in a company in my town. Chances are this is repeated, in some form at other, at businesses across the United States. The company rewards employees for consistently exceeding annual profit goals. When the company exceeds profit goals by a predetermined percentage, the company treats all of its employees and their spouses to either a Caribbean cruise or an exotic vacation in Mexico.

The employees win the company-sponsored trip almost every time it's offered. They work together and do what it takes to succeed. This can mean long hours and overtime on weekends. Scrap materials and defects in quality are kept to a minimum. Peer pressure exists to keep all employees working as productively as possible. Employees who work at this company are proud of their jobs and proud to be associated with the company. The stress to exceed annual profit goals and win the trip works out to everybody's advantage. This type of atmosphere creates a win-win situation. Management is happy, the stockholders are happy, and the employees are happy.

Certainly not all companies can offer cruises and vacations to all employees. The gist of it is that the company promotes a healthy work environment, and productivity is maximized. This principle can be applied to all businesses. Make your employees happy, and they will repay your efforts. Build an atmosphere of distrust and dispute, and your employees will also repay those efforts—and nobody will win.

CORPORATE POLICIES AND PROCEDURES

Reducing violence in the workplace starts at the top of the corporate ladder, but it must involve everyone. Every employee in the workplace, from the chief executive officer to the night janitor, has a responsibility to him- or herself, to coworkers, to the company, and to the community to reduce violence in the workplace. Just as it takes all of the members of a work group to produce a complex piece of equipment, the entire team of employees must make a solid commitment to ensure a safe and secure working environment. Although each employee will have a different role to play, all roles are increasingly important.

Starting with the chief executive officer, president, team leader, or whoever leads the way in managing the company, a commitment must be made to provide protection for all employees from intimidation, harassment, threats, and violence. Without this commitment, all other efforts will surely fail due to lack of managerial support. Managerial support must be strong and unquestionable. This commitment does not necessarily mean that the managerial staff will become involved in investigating each case of possible harassment. It does mean that management will support the staff that is charged with conducting the investigation. A written public statement shows support for those who must decide how to deal with employees who violate the norms of expected social behavior.

Give every employee in the company, including all new hires, a copy of the company policy regarding workplace harassment, intimidation, and threats. Translate the policy into whatever languages your employees speak. Require each employee to read and sign the statement, and keep a copy of the signed statement in the employee's personnel file. Later, if the employee is found to have violated the policy, you will be better able to justify discipline, up to and including termination. (See the box "Corporate Policies and Procedures.")

To assist you in establishing your own written statement on workplace violence, a sample policy statement is provided. (See the

---

Corporate Policies and Procedures

- Top management is responsible for reducing workplace violence.
- A written policy prohibiting violence, harassment, and threats must be clearly posted and communicated to all employees.
- Policies and procedures relative to workplace violence must be written, taught, and followed.
- All employees have a responsibility to assist in providing a safe and healthful work environment free of all known hazards.
- All employees who are found to have violated this policy should face disciplinary action, up to and including termination.

---

box "Sample Policy Statement on Workplace Violence.) The statement can, and should, be modified to meet the unique needs of your organization.

LEGAL ASPECTS OF A SECURE WORK ENVIRONMENT

Furnishing a safe and secure work environment is not only the right thing to do, it's also a legal responsibility. The failure to provide a secure work environment could lead to civil or criminal liabilities. The legal repercussions could affect both the company and the people responsible for providing a safe work environment.

After any death in the workplace, regardless of the reasons for the death, among the first people to visit the work site will be officials from the Occupational Safety and Heath Administration (OSHA). If the death was a result of the employer's failure to provide a safe and healthful work environment, the company could

---

Sample Policy Statement on Workplace Violence

It is the policy of [Name of Business] to provide a safe and secure work environment for all employees. We aim to provide a work atmosphere that promotes trust, fairness, and achievement for employees. [Name of Business] expressly prohibits all acts of intimidation, harassment, and threatening behavior.

Employees have a responsibility to themselves, other employees, and the company to report all incidents of intimidation and harassment as well as other safety- and security-related matters occurring in the workplace. All reports will be thoroughly investigated by management staff. Any employee found to be in violation of this policy will be subject to disciplinary action, including possible dismissal.

---

face severe fines. The personnel responsible for providing a safe and secure work environment could also be held personally liable for the death. If OSHA finds an individual personally responsible for a workplace death or injury, he or she could face both criminal and civil prosecution. Although rare, jail time and personal fines could result.

In a landmark case, OSHA cited Charter Barkley Hospital in Chicago for failing to provide a safe work environment under OSHA's General Duty Clause, Section 5(a)(1). The citation was issued in September 1993 for not having safeguards in place to protect workers in the psychiatric units from violent patients. Since the citation, the hospital has initiated training programs and other measures to prevent violence in the hospital.

Other potential problems could arise under workers' compensation cases when employees are injured or killed while performing their duties. Employees can file a claim against the company not only for their injury, but also for lost wages, stress disabilities, and permanent losses as a result of their injury.

Some businesses believe that they cannot afford to provide safety-related training and security equipment. However, compare the cost of the training and equipment to that of paying for surgery for a gunshot wound. The surgery and the hospital stay could easily cost $50,000, and this doesn't include the cost of lost wages and permanent disabilities. The final dollar figure will be even higher if an employee or customer dies as a result of an attack.

Negligent hiring lawsuits could surface from employees and their families if a company is found to have not fulfilled its legal responsibilities regarding preemployment screening. Courts have already established that the company has a duty to protect employees and customers from other workers that the company knows, or should have known, posed a risk to others. Employers should conduct preemployment screenings to weed out potential problems.

Allowing a hostile work environment to exist also creates a legal issue for employers. The failure to provide proper supervision has resulted in lawsuits.

REFERENCE

1. H.F. Bensimon, "Violence in the Workplace," *Training and Development Journal* (January 1994): 27.

5

Education and Training

EMPLOYEE EDUCATION

The responsibility for security must rest with all employees. From a security standpoint, the employees are the eyes and ears of the business. They are privy to the conversations taking place in the break rooms, locker rooms, and washrooms. They are the ones who hear the threats, stories, and rumors before managers and security professionals do. When an employee identifies and reports a potential security problem, the problem can be investigated and resolved before it escalates, and losses can be mitigated. Security managers should not overlook employees as a resource for information. Try to tap into this resource. Actively solicit the support and cooperation of your employees in preventing workplace violence.

Every company's overall safety program must include employee training. Employers can expect to be hit with a lawsuit if they fail to provide security- and safety-related training and an employee is injured or killed during an incident of workplace violence. The courts have ruled that employers are responsible for providing employees with a safe and secure work environment.

Employees need to be educated on a variety of security- and safety-related topics. Training for all employees should include general security awareness, personal responsibility to ensure security, and recognizing and responding to aggressive behavior from coworkers, customers, or others at the workplace. Employees who work with money must be taught how to act during and immediately following a robbery. Robbery deterrence should also be taught. The location and operation of alarms should be covered for all employees who work in the vicinity of panic alarms. Employees who may be called on to assist in apprehending a shoplifter must know how to do this in a safe and legal manner. (Robbery training is covered in Chapter 8.)

Educating employees about the signs of potentially aggressive or violent behavior can diminish the likelihood of violence striking your business. Employees need to know what to report and to whom. Employees at all levels of the organization should be taught how to recognize potentially destructive behavior in a disturbed employee *and* how to respond to it. The response should include reporting procedures in both emergency and nonemergency circumstances. Identification is of little use without evaluation and intervention.

Most employees want to do the right thing when it comes to helping maintain a safe facility, but without the proper training, they might react poorly to volatile situations because they do not know what is expected of them. For example, consider an office worker who sees an unauthorized, unfamiliar person wandering around in a restricted area. If the employee does not know what is expected of her, she must decide how to respond to the trespasser. Her possible decisions include the following:

- Ignore the situation.
- Confront the intruder immediately.
- Find another employee and then confront the intruder.

Nationally Recognized Training Services

American Society of Industrial Security, (703) 522-5800

Burns International Security Services, (201) 397-2000

Diebold Inc., (800) 999-3600

Pinkerton Security and Investigation Services, (800) 232-7465

STA International, Inc., (604) 873-3252

USATRECK International, (703) 448-0178

U.S. Training and Development Center, (703) 434-8999

Wackenhut Corporation, (800) 929-5585

- Contact a supervisor or manager.
- Contact building security.
- Contact local law enforcement.

The expected employee response should already have been defined during training. What if the intruder is a young woman with a child who is looking for the rest room? In many instances, calling the police would be an overreaction. However, what if the intruder is a 6'10" man weighing 275 pounds? If employees feel uncomfortable or intimidated by the prospect of confronting a stranger, it is probably best that they don't. Unless you offer employees guidance on whom to call, you leave them in a no-win situation. The decision to act or not to act also depends on the business environment and the associated risks (e.g., a nuclear plant vs. grocery store).

Companies that lack the resources to employ an in-house security or training professional can contract with consultants to conduct the training. (See the box "Nationally Recognized Training Services.") Safety and security training should be conducted for all new employees and should be reviewed at least annually or when a change in job duties occurs. Training review is also very beneficial after any significant incident or threats. Employees should be allowed to provide input into the curriculum since they often have specific concerns. Ample time should be allowed for questions at the end of the program. Instructors should also inform employees that they are available to discuss concerns privately.

In some instances, state laws dictate the extent and frequency of employee security and safety training. Check with your legal counsel about the laws in your area. Consider state-mandated training to be the minimum requirement. Give employees as much training as they need to carry out their job responsibilities in a safe manner. With the recent increased awareness of violence in the workplace and the growing number of regulations that businesses must comply with, it's only a matter of time before all businesses will be required by law to provide security training.

MANAGER AND SUPERVISOR TRAINING

Managers, supervisors, human resource personnel, and security professionals need training on proper identification and intervention techniques. When employees come to management to voice concerns over the behavior of another employee, management personnel must have the knowledge and resources to handle the situation. Policies and procedures should be available on dealing with potentially violent employees and customers, and all managers and supervisors must be thoroughly familiar with these written programs.

Not only must managers and supervisors be able to respond to employee concerns, they must also be able to identify situations that put them at personal risk. In a significant number of violent workplace incidents, employees or former employees return to the work site to get revenge on the person they believe wronged them. Many times, the "wrongdoer" is the person who disciplined or terminated the employee—that is, the manager, supervisor, human resource manager, or union steward.

Managers must know when to contact the crisis intervention team or local law enforcement personnel. The first report of suspicious behavior is usually channeled through frontline supervisors. A manager or supervisor may be the first person on the scene when an employee, customer, or client becomes enraged. Managers and supervisors require specific training to guide them through the crisis. When the situation is controllable, the manager or supervisor must be proficient at defusing aggressive behavior before the hostility escalates. This includes knowing the warning signs that usually precipitate violent behavior. (They are discussed in Chapter 7.)

If violence does erupt, managers, supervisors, and employees need to know evacuation and other procedures. Who will be responsible for ensuring that all employees are accounted for, and how will they do this? As in a fire, employees must be accounted for after an act of workplace violence, and a search must be conducted for those who are missing. Such procedures must be established in advance.

Managers and supervisors must also understand the legal requirements for providing a safe and secure work environment for all employees. They could be held liable for their decisions.

Training should be conducted to educate hiring personnel, including managers and supervisors, about preemployment screening and background checks for new employees. A negligent hiring lawsuit could easily result when the wrong employee is put into a position of trust without the proper background screening. (Negligent hiring and negligent retention are covered in Chapter 6.) The procedures for referring employees to available employee assistance programs or local counseling services should be included in managerial training. With proper referrals to counseling services, many potential problems can be resolved before they become critical or dangerous.

CRISIS INTERVENTION TEAM TRAINING

The crisis intervention team should be composed of the following professionals: the human resource or employee relations manager, the security manager, a psychiatrist or psychologist, and an attor-

Training Topics

Employee Training

- Security awareness
- Overview of workplace violence
- Internal and external threats
- Signs of potentially violent behavior
- Robbery procedures and prevention measures
- Location and operation of alarm equipment
- Access-control measures and ID badges
- Reporting requirements
- Company policies and procedures
- Whom to call for help
- Availability of security and police

Supervisor and Manager Training

Supervisor and manager training consists of all of the topics included in employee training, plus the following:

- Preemployment screening practices
- Employee-assistance programs
- Emergency response and evacuation procedures
- Signs of potentially violent behavior
- Behavioral observation
- Patterns of behavior
- Defusing volatile situations
- Employee adverse action training
- Acting and reacting to employee behavior
- Legal requirements and labor relations
- Employee assistance programs

Crisis Intervention Team Training

At least one team member should study all the above topics. The rest need training in the following:

- Threat evaluation and response
- Team effectiveness
- Business recovery planning

ney who specializes in labor law. Each member of the team offers specialized expertise. The combination of each person's knowledge and experience should put the team in a good position to carry out the responsibilities associated with crisis intervention. All members of the team should be volunteers concerned about workplace violence and have an interest in its prevention and intervention.

At least one person on the crisis intervention team, perhaps the security manager, should be trained on all topics taught to employees, supervisors, and managers. The team must know the extent of the information and training available to the rest of the company.

The three main goals of the team are to

1. Gather and document information regarding the incident, threats, or behavior being investigated
2. Analyze the information gathered
3. Recommend a course of action to the decision makers

Each person on the team should provide input into the evaluation and recommendations. By working together as a team, the group can develop action plans to resolve crises before tragedy strikes. In the event that violence does occur, the team will also be instrumental to the recovery process. Each team member should be trained in his or her role in the business recovery plan.

6

Policies and Procedures

HIRING

As the old computer saying goes, "Garbage in, garbage out." The same concept holds true for the work force. Proper screening, testing, and hiring policies and procedures should be in place at every company to ensure that the best employee is hired to fill an open position. Not only is this good security sense; it's also good business sense. (See the box "Good Hiring Practices.")

Proper screening and background checks on new employees can help prevent workplace violence. Fill an open position in your company as you would fill a child-care position in your home. You would never bring a total stranger into your home and leave him or her unsupervised with your baby. The same should be true for your business. Yet hundreds of times every day across the United States, people hire employees to begin jobs based solely on the information provided on a job application.

Good Hiring Practices

- Ask current employees for recommendations for vacant positions.
- Have each applicant fill out a formal job application.
- Ask for the names and addresses of former employers.
- Request written permission to contact former employers.
- Request written permission to check academic records.
- Question periods of unemployment and declining salaries.
- Prepare well for the interview.
- Ask behavioral questions (that is, "Describe a time when . . .").
- Check personal and professional references.
- Conduct background checks on criminal convictions, driving records, and credit if applicable.
- Do not ask questions that may be illegal (that is, age, marital status, religion, sexual preferences).

Research indicates that one-third of all job applicants falsify their employment applications.[1] These falsifications include everything imaginable. Some applicants make up college degrees and employment information to increase their chances of obtaining a position. Some alter or omit felony convictions, job terminations, and even Social Security numbers to meet their needs.

If you were hiring a person to baby-sit your child, you would use caution and verify the applicant's credibility and credentials before giving away the key to the house. You would contact former employers, and you might drive by the applicant's home to see if it is clean and cared for. You might require the potential child-care provider to produce copies of insurance papers, a driver's license, state certifications, and copies of first aid or cardiopulmonary resuscitation (CPR) certifications. Once you are convinced that the baby-sitter is an honest and reputable person, you might hire him or her on a trial basis until you feel even more certain of the baby-sitter's credentials.

Many businesses don't use the same precautions when filling open positions. Laws vary from state to state on the methods employers can use to conduct background checks on applicants. Some states restrict background investigations until after the person has actually been hired to fill a position. If it is discovered that the applicant falsified the employment application, he or she can be terminated. As an employer, you should know the laws for your state before deciding on the hiring practices you will use. Invasion of privacy can be a very costly mistake for any company. Your options include honesty tests, polygraph tests, and background investigations.

Negligent hiring can also be a very costly mistake. Negligent hiring is a legal doctrine that holds that employers can be held liable when they fail to use reasonable care in choosing an applicant, given the risks associated with the position to be filled. The theory behind this action is that the company must determine—before hiring—that the applicant is not a risk to others given the scope of the position. The employer must check the applicant's background to determine if there is reason to believe that the applicant would be unacceptable in the position.

To illustrate, suppose again that you need to hire a baby-sitter to care for your young child. A candidate who has been convicted of child endangerment or child abuse is probably not someone that you would trust to be alone with your child. Failing to uncover the candidate's history of child endangerment or abuse could constitute negligent hiring. If another candidate had been found guilty of tax evasion, this may or may not affect your hiring decision—unless the candidate was applying for a tax audit position.

Different positions entail different risks. The position of security officer involves a different set of risks than the position of cafeteria attendant. When attempting to determine the risks associated with a position, consider the types of access that the employee has. Will the employee have access to master keys, weapons, vulnerable individuals, private homes, or drugs or other items that require special precautions? Imagine for a moment the potential damage that could be caused by a drug addict acting irresponsibly in a nuclear power plant. Background checks for positions in a nuclear power plant must be thorough. The damages resulting from negligent hiring could affect millions of people.

Other positions that require special consideration are jobs that require the employee to enter another person's home. Examples of these jobs include repair technicians, meter readers, visiting nurses, apartment complex managers and service workers, and police officers. The people who open their doors to admit a company's representative trust that the company has already taken their safety into consideration when it hired the employee. People who unlock their doors for your employee have a right to expect that the employee will act within the boundaries of both the law and the company's policy.

The abundance of laws that exist to protect applicants from invasion of privacy place the employer in a catch-22 situation. As an employer, you must use reasonable care and conduct background checks before hiring an applicant, yet you must be careful in how you conduct these preemployment checks.

Employers are typically very guarded about the information they are willing to provide about former employees because they wish to stay out of court. A very thin line exists between what an employer can and can't, should and shouldn't, do. There are, however, legal ways to conduct checks without the danger of litigation. Consult with your legal counsel before beginning a background check.

There are numerous ways to check up on applicants to determine whether they have falsified the job application and whether they are telling the truth about their general history. The depth of the preemployment investigation should depend on the duties of the position and the risks related to that position.

The Application Form and Résumé

The place to start the screening process is with the application for employment. Every business should use an application form that asks about the applicant's level of education and previous employment. When screening the applicant, investigate periods of unexplained unemployment.

Some applicants leave the job market for perfectly legitimate reasons. Some parents decide to stay home and care for their children. It is also becoming more common for people to stay home and care for elderly parents or other relatives who need constant care. Whatever the case, the applicant should be able to provide a solid reason for the period of unemployment.

When the unemployment cannot be explained, there is cause for concern. During the unexplained period of time, did the applicant obtain money illegally, spend time in jail, or fulfill community service sentencing? Perhaps the applicant didn't work because of laziness or drug or alcohol abuse. If the reason for leaving the job market is valid, the applicant should be willing and able to explain it.

The application form should request information regarding the applicant's prior jobs and salary history for at least the past ten years. Applicants who jump from job to job will probably not last long at your company. Emotional problems may be a reason why the applicant was unable to retain any position for an extended period of time.

For each position held, applicants should be asked why they left the company, and they should be asked for permission to contact the former supervisor. Applicants who say they left a former position due to a personality conflict or an inability to get along with management may be signaling that they lack people skills. Ask open-ended questions to probe for more exact details.

Look also at the applicant's salary history. A history of declining salaries should raise a red flag. Tactfully ask the applicant why he or she is looking for a lower position (or responsibility level) than held before. Investigate the possibility that the applicant may have a condition that diminishes reliability or productivity over time (such as drug or alcohol abuse). Whatever the reason, the applicant should be able to provide an explanation for the decline in salary over the years.

The application form should ask for information about the applicant's educational background. In addition to the schools and colleges attended, applicants should provide the address, telephone number, and dates of attendance for each school. Areas of study, grades, and special activities should also be listed.

For technical or higher-level positions, the hiring decision often rests, at least in part, on the applicant's academic achievement. Exaggerating scholastic achievements is common. Ask applicants to provide an official transcript from each college. The majority of colleges use a seal to mark transcripts as official. A seal that indents the paper, similar to a notary stamp, reduces the applicant's ability to change the grades and then photocopy the result. Contact the registrar's office at all colleges that the applicant attended to find out about the type of stamp used on official transcripts.

Carefully compare the information on the transcripts against the information that the applicant provided on the employment form and résumé. All applicants want to look their best, and some overstate their grades slightly. Rounding grade point averages up a tenth of a percent is typical. Depending on the position, this embellishment might be disregarded. Some applicants may not remember their exact grade point average and will write down what they think it was. When the numbers are close and there is no other reason to suspect dishonesty, a simple explanation from the applicant should suffice.

When a significant discrepancy is present or when other issues of honesty are involved, look closer at the applicant's history and background. If there are major discrepancies, remove the applicant from the list of candidates. For example, an applicant who claims to have a college degree but did not finish college should be dropped from consideration.

When you believe that someone may have falsified the application or résumé, you may want to request a second application. Have the person fill out the second form without referring to any records. Explain that you understand that the applicant might not remember exact dates, addresses, or telephone numbers. The information on the second application will be less detailed than on the first application. This should be expected. When you compare the two applications and the résumé, look for major flaws and omissions.

Every application form should advise the applicant that the falsification of information is grounds for immediate termination of employment. Request permission to contact former employers and conduct a background check to verify information contained on the application.

The Interview

The interview process is designed to discover whether an applicant is qualified and suited for the position available. When the interview is conducted correctly, it provides the interviewer with the opportunity to learn more about the applicant. It also gives the applicant a chance to answer any questions raised about the application form.

Preparation is the key to a successful interview. Take time before the interview to review the duties and responsibilities of the position; look over the job description if available. Then prepare a set of written questions related to the performance of the job. All questions asked should directly correlate to the position for which the applicant is being interviewed. Questions about religion, age, marital status, and the like are illegal and may cause legal problems for the interviewer and the company later.

Take the written list of questions into the interview with you. When writing out the questions, leave plenty of space between them to allow you to take lots of notes. The list will help you stay on track during the interview and will help you avoid questions that may be illegal.

When you meet with the applicant, shake hands and introduce yourself. Help the applicant feel comfortable by breaking the initial tension with small talk about the weather or traffic. You want the applicant to be as comfortable as possible in order to gain a realistic opinion of how that person would operate in the work environment.

A relatively new concept in interviewing involves examining how the applicant behaved in the past. The interviewer asks questions that require the applicant to describe his or her experiences. This leads away from the typical question-and-answer period that all college seniors study during their Interviewing Concepts 101 class. We have all been through interviews in which we were questioned about our biggest fault. The standard answer for that is, of course, "I'm far too dedicated to my job, and I work much, much too hard."

Behavioral interviewing focuses more directly on how the applicant actually behaved in the past. The questions begin with some pretext like the following:

- Tell me of a time when you . . .
- Give me an example of when you . . .
- How did you handle . . .
- When you were presented with . . .
- Before, when you had a problem with . . .

The questions can be modified to elicit a behavioral response indicating to the interviewer how the applicant reacted in a similar set of circumstances. For example, you might say, "Tell me of a time when you and your supervisor had a major disagreement about how a task should be handled." Don't let applicants who claim that they've never disagreed with the boss off the hook. We all know that's impossible!

As an interviewer, you want to know how applicants handled this matter before to get an idea of what to expect from them in the future. Most people have had more than one disagreement with a former employer. Applicants' answers may reflect the most significant or trying episode that they have ever had. How the applicant answers this question may be the key to how this person handles frustration.

If the applicant has initial difficulty answering this question or any other, you can always go back and ask the same question later. The answer is important and definitely worth the wait. The person you hire may stay with the company for many years, and you want to choose wisely.

Take plenty of notes during the interview, and ensure that your notes would stand up in a court of law. Don't make notes on physical appearance or other matters that are expressly prohibited by law. It is a good practice to offer the interviewee the option to review the notes you have taken. Most applicants will pass up the opportunity. Your notes will assist later in the decision-making process.

The Background Check

After the interview has taken place and the candidate list has been narrowed down to one to three people, it's time to start verifying the information provided on the application or résumé and given during the interview. The extent of the background check you perform depends on the type of position to be filled. (See the box "Nationally Recognized Companies That Do Background Checks.")

At a minimum, check with former employers. Due to the possibility of lawsuits, most companies limit the information they sup-

---

Nationally Recognized Companies That Do Background Checks

The Ackerman Group, Inc., (305) 865-0218
American Security and Investigation Services, (415) 597-4500
Burns International Security Services, (201) 397-2000
First Security Systems Corp., (617) 568-8700
Guardsmark, Inc., (901) 522-6000
Pinkerton Security and Investigation Services, (818) 380-8800
Wackenhut Corporation, (800) 929-5585
Wells Fargo Guard Services, (800) 327-4699

ply about former employees to the dates of employment and possibly beginning and ending wages. Some companies do provide additional information, though, so it's worth the effort to ask.

Ask the applicant to list at least three personal and professional references and to provide written approval to contact them. The human resources staff should definitely contact these people. Previous supervisors should also be contacted for reference information. When calling for references, have a list of questions ready and take notes. Ask about statements and incidents that the candidate described during the interview. For example, suppose you asked the applicant, "Tell me of a time when you had two important deadlines due at the same time and you only had enough time to complete one project. How did you handle that?" Suppose the applicant responded,

> Project X and the annual sales figures were both due at three o'clock. At one o'clock, when I realized there was no way to turn them both in on time, I went to my supervisor and explained the situation and let him decide which project should take priority.

Ask the supervisor about that specific incident to determine whether the applicant was honest in describing the incident during the interview. Ask the former supervisor if he would hire the employee again if given the opportunity. He will probably say yes to avoid potential hassles later on. Listen to the tone of his voice, and listen for any signs of hesitation that might indicate a less than honest answer.

TERMINATION

When disciplinary measures fail to provide the necessary results and an employee's unacceptable behavior continues, it is time to terminate the employee. Most managers and supervisors find this aspect of the job one of the hardest to accomplish. When the difficulty of the termination is compounded by the threat of violence from the employee, it becomes much harder.

Regardless of the reason for the termination, the manager, supervisor, and human resource professional must do their homework in advance. Preparation is a key principle when terminating an employee. Knowing in advance that all of the *i*'s are dotted and the *t*'s are crossed will assist you when you call the employee in for that fateful meeting. Not only will preparation help keep you out of court, but it will also help you sleep better at night, knowing that the termination was fully justified.

Fired employees often say that it was not the fact that they were terminated that upset them, but the way the termination was handled. Terminations are never pleasant experiences for either party, but respect and consideration are essential. (See the box "Good Termination Practices.")

When you fire an employee, expect some type of emotional response. Such reactions are expected and normal. These include anger, frustration, disbelief, depression, and hysteria. The employee may move from one emotional outburst to another in a matter of minutes. The range of the emotion may change rapidly and with little notice.

Plan the termination in advance, and prepare all documentation. If human resource professionals are available, they should review the termination package to ensure that the termination is legal and that all of the paperwork is in order. If you suspect that the employee may become violent, notify the security department before the termination meeting. (Additional information on this is provided in Chapter 7.)

Always conduct the termination in a private location, and keep it brief. Tell the employee up front that he or she is being terminated—and why. If company policy dictates that the employee receive a termination letter, provide it right away. Keep the termination letter brief and to the point. If the employee will receive severance benefits, present this information in writing during the meeting.

Terminations should be conducted late in the business day. After the termination, do not allow the employee to return to the work area without an escort. A security officer or the supervisor

---

Good Termination Practices

- Complete all documentation in advance.
- Have the human resource department review the termination package.
- Conduct all terminations in private, near the end of the business day.
- Alert security officers prior to a termination.
- Keep termination meetings brief.
- Retrieve all identification badges, keys, company credit cards, and other company property.
- Cancel computer, voice mail, and any other electronic access privileges.
- Notify employees who need to know (receptionists, etc.).
- Provide additional security for supervisors, managers, or human resource personnel who assisted with the termination.

---

or manager may want to escort the person back to the work area to collect personal belongings. In some companies, the supervisor or manager cleans out the employee's desk and takes any personal belongings to the room where the termination is taking place. The employee is given the opportunity to review the items to see if anything has been overlooked.

During the termination meeting, ask the employee to turn over all keys, access cards, identification badges, company credit cards, and any other company property. If the employee had access to voice mail systems, computer systems, or access systems, access privileges and passwords should be deactivated immediately. When keys are not returned, the doors should be rekeyed to prevent access into the facility. The employee should also be told that he or she is not allowed back onto company property without a prior written appointment with the human resources manager or business owner. Passwords to cylinder locks should also be changed.

Do not subject the terminated employee to the embarrassment of being escorted from the building in front of former co-workers. The employee may specifically ask to remain until most people have left the building. This request should be granted when feasible.

When the threat of violence is a very real possibility, the company can seek a court-issued injunction barring the employee from company property. This injunction can be expanded to help protect those who were instrumental in the employee's termination. An injunction should not be viewed as a cure-all for security measures, however. The former employee may become enraged when served with an injunction. It may intensify his or her anger and make retaliation a more genuine possibility. However, in many jurisdictions the injunction will assist law enforcement officers who intervene during a trespassing incident.

The receptionist must be informed of the termination and of any possibility of danger that may exist. A picture of the employee should be placed where the receptionist and any other employees near open-access doors can see it. Showing a picture once and then taking it away will only be as effective as the receptionist's memory.

Employees sitting near open-access points do not need to know the reason for the termination, only that a significant threat has been made. Information on threats must be communicated to employees who are in access-controlled areas. Receptionists and other employees need to know whether the threat involves guns, knives, or other weapons. The failure to provide this information puts the affected employees in a risky position, and the failure to disclose the risk could land the business in a lawsuit if violence occurs.

Additional security protection should be provided for the supervisor, manager, and human resource people who were involved in the termination. This may include walking them to and from their cars, monitoring their visitors and deliveries, and perhaps even providing security recommendations for their homes.

Even when an employee's indentification badge has been returned and all access privileges have been canceled, caution should still be exercised. On December 7, 1988, David Burke, a discharged employee from USAir, boarded a plane scheduled to fly from Los Angeles to San Francisco. He used his employee identification badge to bypass security at the airport. Burke shot his former boss during the flight, then went to the cockpit of the plane and shot both the pilot and the copilot. The plane crashed, killing all forty-three people on board. USAir claims that it did receive Burke's identification badge when it terminated his employment, but it was possible for an employee to have more than one badge.

EMPLOYEE-ASSISTANCE PROGRAMS

Employee-assistance programs were first developed in the 1940s to help employees who were dealing with alcohol abuse. Often, employees who successfully recovered from alcohol addiction were designated by the employer as on-site counseling representatives. They provided support and help to other employees with alcohol addictions. When problem employees became too much of a nuisance for the employer to deal with and the in-house counseling failed, they were simply fired and replaced.

As time went on, employers began to understand that discharging problem employees was not an effective or cost-efficient solution. The emergence of labor unionization, termination policies, and increased termination litigation forced U.S. business and industry to develop a more proactive and economical manner in which to salvage employees who would have otherwise been fired.

The first of today's employee-assistance programs (EAPs) varied in form and technique. Some management philosophies dictated a "fix it or be fired" approach. The employee was formally put on notice that management knew a problem existed, and he or she was warned that continued employment was contingent on the problem being immediately corrected. For employees already facing problems, this do-or-die approach was of little value. It didn't take long for these EAP counselors to gain a reputation as the grim reapers of employment.

As time went on, business professionals learned that employee problems had an even larger and more significant impact on the company's profit statement than they had suspected. Employees were bringing more problems to work with them than alcohol- and drug-related difficulties. Studies showed that a work force suffering from stress caused by a multitude of emotional problems costs companies huge amounts of money. The company's survival could be determined by the mental well-being of the workers.

Today's EAPs were developed to help management reduce the costs associated with increased tardiness, absenteeism, and sick time; rising health-care and workers' compensation expenses; and other costs related to poor job performance. Throughout the years, the role of EAPs has evolved to encompass more of the problems that workers face, including substance abuse, uncontrolled stress, family and marital problems, and employment-related difficulties. In the counseling role, the recovering alcoholic was replaced with clinical professionals in the fields of social work, psychology, and counseling.

Three main types of EAPs exist today: telephonic, in-house, and purchased services. In the first type of service, employees are given a toll-free number to call whenever they want to receive assistance. The telephone is answered somewhere in the United States by a person who makes an initial assessment of the employee's problem and refers the employee to a local agency that contracts with the national EAP. Telephonic services are often the least expensive and least effective programs available.

Many large companies have begun to provide employees with in-house EAP services. They retain a trained professional staff on location, and these counselors work very closely with both the management and the employees on problem resolution. Many of the companies that have switched to this type of program have experienced tremendous success. Unfortunately, small and medium-size companies usually do not have the resources to offer an in-house EAP.

The last type of EAP is purchased services. With purchased services, the company contracts with a mental-health provider in the local area to furnish EAP services. Employers generally have a choice of paying a flat fee per year per employee or paying for the services used. The type of program set up typically depends on the needs of the company. Purchased services are often the best option for companies that want to contract for employee-assistance counseling.

A relatively new concept in employee-assistance programs employs corporate chaplains or other members of the clergy as counselors. This practice has been widely used in the military and in hospitals. Many large corporations are also using clergy services to assist employees with problems and to assist management in defusing potentially volatile situations. Substantial growth in this field is expected as more corporations discover the value of providing these services to their employees.

The type of EAP service obtained depends on the company's management philosophy, the level of employee need, and the company's financial resources. Small businesses and companies with limited financial resources may elect to join forces with other companies in the same position and negotiate a shared contract for services.

The two main objectives of any EAP are to help employees resolve problems that affect their well-being and to turn problem employees into productive employees in a cost-efficient manner. It is far less expensive to rehabilitate an employee with poor performance due to life pressures than to interview, hire, and train a new worker.

Federal laws protect employees with certain physical and mental disorders. The Americans with Disabilities Act (ADA) requires employers to make reasonable accommodations for workers with handicaps. In many cases, the employer must also make accommodations for employees who are suffering from mental illness. A major implication of this law is that employers now have a duty to assist in the rehabilitation of mentally ill employees.

I interviewed Dr. Barbara Murphy in February 1995 to gain her insight into the role that EAPs play in business and industry. Dr. Murphy is the Mental Health Director at Allen Memorial Hospital in Waterloo, Iowa. In addition to other duties, she manages the hospital's EAP purchased-services program. Much of this section reflects Dr. Murphy's observations and recommendations as to the role of EAPs in the overall well-being of workers and the reduction of employee violence.

According to Dr. Murphy, a key factor in developing and maintaining a useful EAP is gaining employee confidence in the program. The effectiveness of an EAP depends on employee utilization of the services. Having a wonderful in-house EAP staffed by professional counselors and others from the mental-health community will be a severe waste of time, money, and talent if employees do not utilize the program.

Employees sometimes fail to take advantage of the services provided by EAPs because they are unfamiliar with the program or believe it to be ineffective. The first roadblock—lack of familiarity with the program—can be resolved by company human resource professionals or management personnel who make a commitment to the well-being of employees. Take advantage of all opportunities to inform employees about the EAP services. There are a number of relatively inexpensive ways to educate and remind employees about the assistance services available, including pamphlets enclosed with paychecks, posters, articles in the company newsletter, and a descriptive summary of services in the benefits manual. Presentations during lunch periods, commonly known as brown-bag lunches, also serve as a tool for employee education.

The EAP representatives should also actively advertise themselves to employees. They should make a very strong effort to make their services known to employees. They can make themselves visible through seminars on topics of interest to workers, such as stress reduction, conflict resolution, and marriage and family issues.

Overcoming employees' perception that the program is ineffective is harder. The first step toward resolving this problem is to find out from employees why they are not using the program. Determining the areas of employee concern with the program will help management and human resource personnel determine which steps are needed to ensure employee confidence in the program. Management may need to look for a different service provider.

Employees may perceive a lack of confidentiality with the in-house or outside program administrators. Employees generally do not want their personal weaknesses or problems to be the topic of discussion at every table in the company cafeteria. Employees who do not believe that their cases will be handled in a confidential manner will not seek assistance through these resources.

The timeliness of services is another reason why employees fail to use EAP services. The assistance program will not work for employees who must wait several weeks for an appointment. According to Dr. Murphy, "It's been proven that people will not wait to resolve a crisis. People who wait six weeks before an appointment will resolve their crisis in another way. Unfortunately, sometimes they do it with a gun." The timeliness of services is thus a very relevant issue.

For employees who display the warning signs of violent behavior, an initial assessment by a mental-health professional must be done as soon as possible. The assessment should take place no more than twenty-four hours after the referral. In almost every incident of employee violence in the workplace, the employee displayed clear warning signs of violent behavior. Many employees flatly told their supervisor of their intentions, then followed through with their threats. These types of incidents can often be prevented. According to Dr. Murphy, employers who ignore employee threats are courting disaster.

When employees who are frustrated believe that they are not being taken seriously and are asked to wait for counseling services, the waiting period only reinforces their feelings of anger and frustration. Some employees decide to show their employer just how serious they really are. The results of this type of display are never beneficial to any of the people involved.

Dr. Murphy suggests several reasons why supervisors, managers, and coworkers ignore the threats of an angry employee. Most people can't even imagine using a gun to solve their problems. When a coworker threatens violence, others don't think the threat is real. It's easier to think that the employee is just blowing off steam or venting frustrations. Even worse, coworkers sometimes ignore the threats because "it's just old Joe, and he's been saying that for years."

In some, if not all, states the employer has the right to demand that an employee seek help from an EAP as a condition of continued employment. Employers considering making a mandatory referral should check with legal counsel to verify their rights. A mandatory referral should not be used in place of other disciplinary actions; instead, referrals should be made in conjunction with disciplinary actions. All actions should be based on job performance.

Once an employee receives a mandatory referral to an EAP, the counselor should work with the employee and the supervisor to achieve the goals required for continued employment. According to Dr. Murphy, the first thing a counselor should do is ask the referred employee to sign a release of information form.

Rules on confidentiality are very strict, and the information that the counselor is entitled to provide to anyone is restricted. The counselor may request permission to tell the employer whether the employee showed up for an appointment, arrived on time, and actively participated in the session. The EAP counselor cannot discuss the specifics of the conversation to the employer, nor can the counselor disclose the recommendations given to the employee. The counselor's role is that of an advocate for the employee. The counselor's loyalty must be to the employee, not the employer, regardless of who pays the bill.

However, the scope of confidentiality does not cover genuine threats made against others, Dr. Murphy says. A counselor or psychologist who determines that the employee is dangerous to others must inform the target of the threats and the local police department. If the counselor believes that a supervisor, manager, or other employee is in danger, the counselor must notify this person. Some state laws may vary slightly, but this is the widely accepted legal practice. The security and human resource departments will not be notified by the EAP professional unless department personnel are the potential victims. However, the targeted employee may report the threat to one or the other of these departments.

If the counselor determines that the danger is directed toward the employee's spouse, he or she should be warned, not the employer. It is mandatory that all counselors, doctors, psychiatrists, and nurses report suspected child abuse. If the counselor has reasonable suspicion that the employee is abusing a child, the counselor must report the incident to law enforcement officials.

In cases in which the employee is in need of counseling but is not a threat to the safety of others, the counselor will begin treatment for the employee. Most EAPs are designed to offer only short-term treatment. The EAP counselor will typically see the employee for one to six sessions, depending on the nature of the problem. This type of counseling approach is often referred to as *problem focused*. During the initial counseling session, the counselor assesses the situation and determines in what areas the employee needs assistance. The counselor then moves into a problem-solving mode to help the employee develop an action plan for resolution.

According to Dr. Murphy, it is sometimes readily apparent that the employee needs long-term help that the EAP program is not designed to provide. In this case, the counselor tries to convince the employee that a problem exists. The EAP professional tries to break down any resistance that the employee may have toward treatment. The counselor tries to show the employee that with additional help, the situation can be resolved or improved. This is the case when the employee is involved in an abusive situation or is dealing with drug- or alcohol-related problems.

In some situations, the counselor may believe that the employee's problems are caused by a medical condition. In this case, the counselor refers the employee to a physician for evaluation and treatment. When the employee decides to undergo treatment, the EAP professional works with the employee's health-care provider to ensure that the referral is covered by the employee's medical

---

Nationally Recognized Employee Assistance Programs

EAP, Inc., (313) 583-1110
Employee Assistance Services, Inc., (800) 448-4434
EPT, (800) 223-2271
Lexington Group, (800) 676-HELP
Occupational Health Centers of America, Inc., (800) 523-0591
Phoenix Group, (800) 336-2204
Priority Systems, (908) 654-6199

---

insurance policy. If the employee does not have medical coverage, the EAP counselor tries to refer the employee to a local agency that provides services on a sliding-fee basis. Whatever the nature or the origin of the employee's problem, the EAP professional's goal is to assist the employee in becoming a fully productive and stable person again.

Dr. Murphy suggests that in cases in which the job or the supervisor is the source of the employee's problems, the counselor may recommend that the employee consider transferring to another department or evaluating other employment opportunities. The counselor should help the employee to explore all options. The counselor should never advise clients on a course of action. Instead, the counselor should help them identify the options that best serve their needs. In a situation like this, a transfer or new job is probably best for the employer as well. The employer will be better off without an angry or disgruntled employee.

Dr. Murphy recommends that all employers who offer an EAP survey their employees to find out how they view the program and whether, if they had a need, they would take advantage of EAP services. "An EAP is not a good deal if it doesn't do anything. Just like anything else, if it's on sale and you don't need it and it doesn't do anything for you, it's no sale." Shop around before contracting with an EAP agency. See the box "Nationally Recognized Employee-Assistance Companies.")

The EAP profession has grown rapidly, and not all service providers who bid on a contract are equipped to provide the services that a company and its employees need. Dr. Murphy encourages employers who are considering contracting for EAP services to ask the following questions:

1. Is the EAP agency familiar with local conditions and local service providers?
2. Does the agency have experience with similar companies and similar employees?
3. Can the agency provide letters of recommendation?
4. What type of paperwork can the company expect to receive from the agency, and what is the frequency of reporting (monthly, quarterly, annually)?
5. Can the agency provide in-house training, and if so, what types of training programs can it provide?
6. Does the agency provide a twenty-four-hour crisis line?
7. What range of providers does the agency work with?
8. What is the cost of the agency's services?
9. Does the agency work with insurance carriers on referrals?

INTERVENTION AND ACTION PLANS

As discussed earlier, every company should have a written policy statement that reflects a no-tolerance level for harassment, intimidation, threats, or violence of any kind against employees, customers, or visitors. Written guidelines must exist to assist supervisors and managers in confronting and resolving perceived and real conflicts. In large corporations, a specialized team may be available to handle the intervention process. In smaller businesses, the owner or manager may be the only immediate resource available to employees who feel threatened. Whichever the case, knowing and deciding in advance which actions are necessary to deal with potential problems will help speed up resolution with a minimal disruption of operations.

The initial notice of a potential problem will most likely come from a concerned or threatened employee. One or more employees may notify management when they believe that the actions of a disgruntled employee are no longer tolerable. It is likely that the employees have been dealing with this employee for a long time and are no longer willing to handle the situation themselves. Employees often hesitate before reporting an incident. They may believe they are overreacting to the disgruntled employee, or they may not want to cause the employee additional problems. Regardless of the reason for waiting before filing a complaint, care should be used not to discourage the employees. Their hesitation is based on concerns that are real to them.

Education is one of the best tools management can use to diminish the risks of workplace violence. All employees—from the factory welder to the supervisor—must know how to recognize a coworker who is an explosion waiting to happen. Employees must also feel comfortable reporting incidents and individuals to management without the fear of reprisal from either the dysfunctional employee or management staff. In some large companies, the human resources department has a hot line or voice mail system through which concerned employees can leave anonymous messages.

In today's workplace, where everybody seems to be having to make more from less, managers and supervisors may feel perturbed at having to investigate a harassment or intimidation claim. They may feel from the beginning that even if a significant concern is warranted, human resources or another department may sweep the entire incident under the rug without ever confronting the employee. They may believe that any intervention on their part is an exercise in futility and that the investigation and investment of their time and resources would be wasted.

Employees who sense these types of feelings or have actually found this to be the case in the past will be reluctant to voice concerns over another employee's behavior. When a single employee or group of employees feels threatened, immediate action must be taken to resolve the situation, or valued employees will themselves become increasingly unproductive or will quit their jobs in fear of their safety and well-being.

All cases reported to management must be fully investigated in a timely manner. The reporting employees should be treated with respect and consideration during the investigation. Once a threat is reported, the team responsible for threat evaluation and intervention should meet. The members of this team may include the human resources manager, the security manager, the employee's manager or supervisor, union representatives, EAP professionals, a psychologist, and in some cases, local law enforcement officials. The size of the team depends on the resources available to the business. In large companies, all of these people may be available but called on only after the initial evaluation has been completed.

In smaller businesses, security, human resources, and EAP representatives may not be available. The owner/manager should consider contacting outside agencies for assistance in the evaluation. When local law enforcement officials are informed of a problem, the company must take responsibility for ensuring that the responding officers understand the urgency of the situation.

The responding agency must know all of the facts involved, not just what the company would like to disclose. Some companies feel a need to protect the employee's privacy or fear causing additional problems for both the employee and the company by bringing in an outside agency. Once a threat has been made, however, secrecy almost becomes a moot point. Because an arrest may not always be made as a result of the first incident, the local police officials must at least document the incident. The documented history will assist both the company and law enforcement officials if additional incidents occur.

Not all response team members need to be experts, but they do need to be trained on identifying, evaluating, and dealing with aggressive behaviors. All team members must be familiar with the company policy on intimidating behavior and the company's intervention and action plan for dealing with threats of violence or harassment.

Once a report has been made, the response team interviews the person who came forward to determine the exact circumstances in which the threat or behavior occurred. When a verbal threat is involved, the exact wording of the threat can be an important indicator of the employee's intention. The team also determines whether this was an isolated or ongoing event. When a history of past incidents exists, record as many details as possible but concentrate on the latest or most significant incident.

Ask for the names of witnesses or others who may have knowledge of the incident being reported. The reporting employee may be reluctant to provide a list of other employees for fear of his or her identity (or the complaint itself) becoming known. Reassure the employee that all conversations and interviews will remain confidential. To assist in maintaining confidentiality, conduct all meetings away from the immediate work area. If the building is small or privacy is not readily available, conduct all interviews away from the work site.

Determine whether the threat was aimed at the reporting employee, another worker, a manager or supervisor, or the company as a whole. Ask the reporting employee about his or her relationship with the disgruntled employee, especially if the threat was aimed directly at the reporting employee. If it becomes apparent that the two employees had a romantic relationship before the threat and that the relationship is the cornerstone of the threat, intervention is still required. The workplace is now involved and, with that, the safety of all employees. Ignoring a seemingly personal problem could be a costly mistake.

All parts of this interview must be documented. The documentation will aid others who are required to assist in the intervention. It will also be easier to justify discipline in future incidents when this information is documented in the employee's personnel file. In a worst-case scenario, the documentation can be used as evidence in a future lawsuit. Documentation will show which actions the company took to help resolve the conflict.

Once the initial interview has been completed, the severity of the threat must be determined. If, after an initial interview, there is cause for concern, other witnesses or involved employees should be interviewed. Ideally, all employees should be interviewed by the same person.

The employee's work history should be examined. Items to pay particular attention to include situations in the past in which the employee was unable to deal effectively with counseling or coaching. When the employee has a history of violence against family members, coworkers, other people, or animals, extra security measures may be needed to protect the employees being interviewed as well as the interviewer.

Contact local law enforcement officials if the threat is substantiated during the interviews. If law enforcement officials become involved, they may be willing to provide information regarding past arrests or incidents involving the employee. Some police departments have experts on staff who can help in the evaluation process.

When evaluating the threat, consider the following factors:

- Does the employee have the means to carry out the threat?
- Does the employee have a known history of violent behavior?
- What is the employee's typical behavior?
- Which risk factors can be associated with the employee's behavior?
- What other warning signs of violent behavior has the employee exhibited in the past?

Examine the employee's original job application to find out if he or she has a military background. Ask those who are being interviewed whether the investigated employee has been known to carry or own weapons.

When the intervention team believes the threat to be nothing more than blowing off steam or "talking big" in front of coworkers, the employee must still be counseled about the behavior. Perhaps the employee did not realize the effect of his or her behavior on other people. In this day and age, people lose their sense of humor quickly when they become the recipient of threats.

Security personnel should be made aware of the counseling session in advance. Follow the techniques discussed in Chapter 7 during the meeting with the disgruntled employee. In countless cases of workplace violence, nobody ever talked to the violent employee about his or her behavior before the incident. The goal in talking to employees accused of intimidating, harassing, or threatening others is to change their behavior. Referral to an EAP or local counseling program may be all that is needed. Such employees need to realize that their future employment depends on their behavior and that they alone are responsible for changing their behavior.

According to one expert, "If an employee's threats appear to be a prelude to some more drastic acts of violence, you can either rehabilitate him or terminate his employment." Rehabilitation means helping the person "get his head on straight and come back to work. Often referring the potentially dangerous employees to a traditional employee-assistance program is enough. Their behavior may stem from alcoholism or drug abuse, and an EAP counselor can suggest a treatment program that could solve the problem."[2]

During the counseling session, advise the employee being investigated that the company is concerned about his or her behavior and that an investigation is being conducted. Give the employee a copy of the company policy on intimidating and harassing behavior. Ensure that the employee understands the company policy and the relationship between future misconduct and possible termination.

If possible, without revealing the identify of the complainant, ask the employee for his or her interpretation of the comments or actions under investigation. Give the employee ample time to explain. Listen and take notes. Write down what the employee actually says, not what you think the employee means. Because taping the conversation involves legal issues that vary from state to state, do not try this before seeking advice from your legal counsel.

When concluding the interview, let the employee know what to expect next. As with any employee counseling session, the employee should leave the room with a clear understanding of what is expected and how long he or she has to achieve these performance objectives. It is always a good idea to provide this list to the employee in writing. A copy should also be kept in the employee's personnel file.

Many companies allow the employee to go home after the meeting. This allows the employee time to think about the discussion and try to make sense of it. This also affords the employee privacy and keeps him or her away from coworkers. Angry employees sometimes try to return to the workplace to recount their side of the story to any employee who is willing to listen. Without a doubt, this results in a disruption of business operations. In addition, the employee who initiated the complaint may feel vulnerable and uncomfortable with the situation. Other employees who support the investigated employee may actually instigate additional threats.

If a very serious or immediate threat is thought to exist, inform security personnel about the meeting, and provide enough details so they can respond accordingly. In too many companies, managers are so concerned about a breach of confidentiality that they fail to supply pertinent details to people who really have a need to know. Effective security measures can only be initiated when the security department knows exactly what it's dealing with.

Decide on the actions to be followed when a significant danger is present. Will the employee be discharged, and if so, under what conditions? Companies have used various measures to make the termination more beneficial and less painful for the employee. Some companies offer employees large bonuses to leave the company quietly and without conflict. Such decisions must be made independently by the businesses involved. Some companies have offered better separation packages and benefits. Severance pay and benefits have been extended to help employees feel less angry about their termination. A company that has the means available should offer access to a counseling program and a job-placement referral service.

SECURITY PROCEDURES

Integrating workplace security policies and practices helps managers reduce the risk of workplace violence. Because not every company can afford, or indeed wants, an armed security officer at every door, security measures must be broken down into manageable and affordable pieces. The security measures required depend on the actual risk of violence occurring in the workplace.

Risk identification is based on a multitude of factors, each of which must be examined to determine its applicability to the environment in which the business operates. Just as it doesn't make sense to provide a safe for a child's lemonade stand, it also doesn't make sense to leave all of the doors open at a coin-minting operation.

One of the most useful tools for determining the level of risk that a business faces is the security audit. There are many reputable companies that specialize in providing security audit services. For those who lack a background in security, contracting with an auditing agency may be far less expensive and time consuming than trying to complete an audit themselves. The local chamber of commerce should provide guidance in choosing a local firm with a good reputation.

With a comprehensive security audit program, the security manager or other responsible person can analyze areas of potential risk (and potential liability) and compare those risks to the preventive measures in place. The review should look at past incidents of security violations and examine them to calculate both the actual and potential damages from such incidents.

Do not ignore future threats just because they have never occurred. Identifying the potential for problems is a key factor for preventing problems later. The audit form should also be updated to reflect changes in risk factors as they develop. New businesses or housing developments in the area can significantly change the amount of traffic for the company, hence changing the risks involved with doing business in a given area.

Types of Threats

Internal Threats	External Threats
Abusive nonviolent employees	Former employees
Disgruntled violent employees	Disgruntled customers
Employee theft	Family members
Employee sabotage	Domestic abuse
Harassment or intimidation	Robberies
Sexual harassment or assault	Bomb threats
Disgruntled vendors	Kidnapping
	Random crime and violence
	Assault/rape

The security audit can also be useful in determining whether budgeted security dollars are being utilized to their full potential. Risks that were a major concern five years ago may not top the list of priorities today. The budget must be reviewed to ensure that issues of importance are being addressed. The money spent to provide some security services might better be spent to train employees.

Risks should be examined in relation to the types of people capable of causing the damage. Just as the motivations for violence vary, so do the security measures necessary to prevent violence. Violence can erupt from current and former employees, their families, customers, and criminals. Each of these groups must be guarded against with various security measures. Some measures will help protect against all groups; other measures will protect only against one category.

Threats can be broken down into two broad categories: internal and external. (See the box "Types of Threats.") People who are already inside of the facility or who gain access without question are considered internal threats. People who must gain entry through the main entrance area or by overcoming physical barriers (such as breaking a window) are considered external threats. Some threats may fall under either category. For example, assault can originate from internal or external sources.

Once the audit has been completed, do not put it in a drawer to collect dust. The audit itself will not correct problem areas. This is where many audits fail. Work still needs to be done after the initial identification procedure. Knowing about possible problems does not prevent the problems from occurring. The failure to follow through after an audit could lead to legal problems if employees, customers, or visitors are injured or killed because of a problem that management knew about but did not address. The victims of workplace violence will have an easy case of negligence when they can prove that management ignored pertinent security problems.

Resources—both people and funding—should be allocated to correct deficiencies in a manner that produces the greatest reduction in security risks to people. Risks to human life should be addressed before issues of property damage. Property insurance can go a long way toward restoring a building loss, but there is no policy available that will restore a human life.

Threat management tactics can be divided into two broad categories: internal and external. Sample tactics are listed in the "Threat Management" box. Many of the items listed under "External Threat Management" also apply to managing internal threats.

Access Control

Physical barriers are among the measures that can be used to prevent external threats from entering the workplace. Examples of external threats include family members, customers, some vendors, and robbers. (Robbery prevention and performance objectives during a robbery are covered in Part III.)

Current employees, some vendors, and service contract personnel typically have a wide range of access to most facilities. They can often gain admission through side doors with electronic card-

---

Threat Management

Internal Threat Management
Security officers
Company policy
Developed procedures
Duress alarms
Employee training
Supervisor/management
  training
Identification badges
Human resources support
Employee-assistance
  programs
Reporting hot line
Recovery plans

External Threat Management
Security officers
Door locks/electronic
  access
Duress alarms
Visitor access controls
Exterior lighting
Closed-circuit television
  systems
Fences and gates
Signs and warnings
Registration logs

---

key access or with a passkey issued by the business. Once they are inside the facility, internal measures are needed to ensure that the security of the facility is maintained. Many of these measures rest with the human resources and security departments.

Photo identification badges should be used to control access by employees, visitors, and guests. The different types of badges available vary considerably in price and quality. Temporary tags range from disposable labels to badges that change physically upon expiration. The latter might expire after a number of hours or days or even when exposed to direct sunlight. Badge features should be proportional to the amount of risk present.

Every employee should be issued an identification badge on the first day of employment. Badges should be replaced when they become outdated or damaged. Current pictures should always be used. Employees who change their name because of marriage, divorce, or for some other reason should be required to obtain an updated identification badge within a specified period of time.

Company policy should dictate that employees wear the identification badge at all times while in the facility. When only some employees wear their identification badges, the effectiveness of the system is reduced to near zero. Security officers, supervisors, and managers should be instructed to counsel employees who do not wear their identification badges, and violations of the rule should be dealt with as performance issues.

Information about the employee may be added to the reverse side of the badge. This information can include just about anything the company chooses, such as security color codes, access levels, medical conditions, height, weight, and other physical characteristics, and Social Security or employee identification number. Bar coding this information will offer confidentiality for those who do not want their numbers publicly displayed.

Smaller companies that lack the means to purchase identification-badge equipment can consult with local photography studios, which can often produce identification badges at a very reasonable fee. Printing shops can assist in printing the cards used for the badges.

In larger companies, employees should be trained to be cautious with people in the facility who are not wearing identification badges. Identification awareness and procedural training for possible violations should be included in employee training. Intruders should be reported to security personnel without hesitation. The general employee population is not privy to immediate information regarding terminated employees. Just because a person was employed at the company earlier in the day doesn't mean that he or she is still on the payroll at quitting time.

Employees and others who attempt to gain access to the facility without displaying proper identification should be directed to the main entrance or whatever entrance the general public uses. The receptionist or security officer on duty should be able to verify employment and issue a temporary identification badge to current employees. When company personnel do not feel comfortable con-

(COMPANY NAME)

REGISTRATION LOG

Badge #	Date	Name	Company	Time in	Time out	Escort

Figure 6–1   Sample registration log.

fronting an unauthorized person, they should contact security personnel immediately to report the intruder. Security officers should investigate the unauthorized entry immediately.

Some employees may view the identification badge as a daily hassle, but managers must support and enforce the company policy requiring the badge. The badge itself should be treated as the employee's authorization to enter and remain in the building.

A registration book must be present at all doors available for public access. In smaller offices, this would most likely be in the reception area. The sample visitor registration form shown in Figure 6–1 can be modified to meet the specific needs of a location. The extent of information gathered on the registration log depends on the level of security desired. Some companies require that all visitors, vendors, and guests be fingerprinted upon arrival. Although fingerprinting is not essential for visitors at most locations, this example does show how security measures can be instituted to meet risk needs.

The registration book requires visitors to supply particular information, such as their name, the date and time of visit, the company they represent (when applicable), and who they are there to see. When escorts are required, they should also write their name in the registration book. When numbered badges are issued, the badge number should be recorded. Visitors to the facility should be required to sign out and return their visitor tag when leaving the building. They should also be required to leave by the same entrance as they arrived.

The registration log serves as a permanent record of people entering the business. Pages in the registration log should be removed each day to avoid potential confidentiality issues. Vendors or competitors may try to view the registration log to determine who has been visiting the company.

Physical Security

Duress, or panic, alarms should be installed in areas where customer or visitor contacts occur. They should be installed in such a way that the employee can activate the alarm unobtrusively. The alarms should be linked with either a private monitoring station or with the local police department.

Panic alarms should also be installed in the offices of managers and human resource personnel who might be targeted for assault by customers or current or former employees. Conference rooms and other areas used for employee grievance hearings should also contain panic alarms. Alarms installed in these offices should be linked to the security office, secretary's desk, or another area that is always occupied by a responsible employee. The employees in these areas must be trained on the procedures to follow when the alarm is activated. Contacting the police or the security department should be included in the procedures. (Additional information on duress alarms appears in Chapter 8.)

Safes should be provided in areas in which employees exchange cash with the public. Employees should be instructed to deposit cash receipts either at designated time intervals or whenever a specific amount of cash is present in the register. Do not give attendants the combination to the safe.

Signs and warnings can also help provide security. Signs are reasonably inexpensive and semipermanent. Many companies 'advertise' the security measures active in their building at entrances. Warning labels such as "Premises protected by surveillance cameras" may encourage the would-be robber to search for a less secured target. Other signs can be used to direct all visitors and vendors to the main entrance. Other signs useful for preventing robberies include "No cash carried," "All cash deposited immediately into safe," and "Security guards on duty."

Interior and exterior lighting should also be viewed as a security measure to prevent crime from occurring on or near the premises. On the inside of the building, all stairways, elevators, and any other areas that might be vulnerable for lone employees should have adequate lighting as well as an emergency backup lighting system.

The exterior areas of the building—including entryways, receiving areas, parking areas, and walkways—should be well illuminated. Burned-out light bulbs should be replaced regularly. Other areas, such as shrubs and trash bins, that might provide an assailant cover should also be either removed or lit enough to make hiding difficult.

Security equipment should make unauthorized entry into the facility more difficult and detection of trespassers easier. Security officers should respond to suspicious activities, threats, and assaults. They should stand by on terminations, be present at layoffs, and assist in controlling picketing lines at strikes. Security managers should assist in the evaluation of threats. Many of the services that security officers perform are reactive rather than proactive in nature.

Security Management

Managing a security staff is similar to managing other staffs. The security manager must deal with the typical issues of absenteeism, illness, vacations, poor performance, and the like. However, a security staff has enough unique features to make the job a challenging one for even the most practiced manager. The security manager must also deal with such issues as continued security coverage over holidays and weekends. The use of force, specialized training, legal issues, and staff retention and boredom are also issues that the security manager must address.

A communication system must be established that all security officers can easily use without elaborate skills. Systems that may work include voice mail or the exchange of written notes. An integral part of any security department is the log reports that security officers should be required to fill out for every shift. Security officers should be trained to write complete and accurate reports on every incident that occurs on their shift.

Training

A rule of thumb for every security department should be to train, train, and retrain. Security officers who lack proper training can cost a company substantially more than any training program conducted. To hire a lawyer to defend against the charge of negligent security training can cost big bucks, and settlements and punitive damages can range in the millions of dollars.

Before establishing a training program, it is a good idea to ask your legal counsel to advise on the areas most commonly targeted for litigation and to specify any training required by state law. These topics should be the minimum requirements of the program. When security officers carry weapons, your company's insurance carrier may be able to assist in determining training needs in addition to those imposed by state law. (See the box "Security Training Topics.")

Once you have identified the training topics, develop a training topic calendar. Classes that need to be repeated periodically

---

Security Training Topics

- Blood-borne pathogens
- Bomb threats
- Building safety
- Cardiopulmonary resuscitation (CPR) and first aid
- Dealing with the public
- Handling aggressive and violent behavior
- Patrol techniques
- Report writing
- Search and seizure
- Self-defense
- Weapon retention and control

---

should be kept on the training calendar on an annual or quarterly basis, whichever is applicable.

Security is a small piece of the overall picture when it comes to preventing workplace violence. Security personnel, practices, and equipment can do a lot to provide protection to employees, visitors, and customers. However, security measures are much more effective when they are combined with a wide range of additional company policies and procedures that support security services.

REFERENCES

1. Mickey Veich, "Uncover the Resume Ruse," *Security Management* (October 1994): 75.

2. B. Filipczak, "Armed and Dangerous at Work." *Training* (July 1993): 42.

III

During Workplace Violence

7

Threatening Behavior

INTIMIDATION AND THREATS

Perhaps some readers have had their life threatened by a violent act or have been threatened at some level by the actions of another human being. Indeed, most people have, at least once in their life, felt threatened with kicks, punches, retaliation, or household items flying past them at a high velocity. For those who have felt the pain and fear of a hostile environment, I offer my empathy and support. For those who have not felt threatened, I sincerely hope you never do.

Intimidation is a terrible thing to feel. The victim of intimation is often a spouse, child, parent, or coworker of a person who does not realize the extent of his or her actions.

Individuals use intimidating or threatening behavior as a means of gaining control over other people or situations. Because intimidation is a common control method that has existed since the beginning of civilization, it must in some way be effective for the abuser.

Those who use intimidation to control others may never know the true results of their actions. They fail to recognize the detrimental effect that their behavior has on those around them. Many times, though, they do know the results of their actions and are looking for a specific response in another person's behavior. The desired response may be fright, terror, panic, compliance, obedience, or submission.

Employees who feel the effects of intimidation or harassment need an immediate resolution of this situation. If the problem is not resolved, the company, the community, and the victim's family will also be added to the victim list. All will eventually suffer the consequences of this unacceptable behavior.

The victim of intimidation or harassment can use certain methods to regain control over the incident. These methods should be initiated after the first episode of intimidation or harassment. For employees, the first line of defense is to report suspicious or violent behavior to their immediate supervisor. If the intimidation included an immediate threat, local police officials should be summoned without hesitation. Employees have a right to be protected from physical harm by everyone, including customers, fellow employees, managers, and family members.

Guidelines for responding to intimidation vary according to the situation. It is always better to overreact and be on the side of safety. Remember, the intimidation and threats affect not only the recipient, but every employee, customer, and bystander in the area. Customers who perceive your company as a place where intimidation is tolerated will take their business elsewhere.

Intimidation often starts with comments, looks, or other behavior that the recipient may not recognize as abusive until it becomes intolerable. The abuse may begin with verbal intimidation, cruel jokes, and negative comments and then expand to include other controlling and abusive actions. The recipient may only gradually become aware of the control that the abuser has over his or her well-being. The victim may have a difficult time deciding when and where to draw the line on what is permissible.

Company policy must dictate that no form of intimidation or harassment will be tolerated at any level of the organization. The policy must also state that all reported incidents of intimidation will be thoroughly investigated and that disciplinary action will be taken when needed. A sample policy statement is included in Chapter 4.

DEALING WITH AGGRESSIVE OR INTIMIDATING BEHAVIOR

Handling aggressive or intimidating behavior is definitely not on every manager's top-ten list of things he or she wants to do, but there comes a time when virtually all managers must confront a person who acts in an aggressive or intimidating manner. Often, this is a person whose behavior has been ignored for a long time. The anxiety of dealing with this person has caused the manager to postpone the inevitable.

Remember that in the overwhelming majority of cases, aggressive and hostile behavior does not result in violence. However, research does indicate that if people are trained on reacting to aggressive and intimidating behavior, they are much better able to handle situations involving aggression and their reaction time to incidents is tremendously enhanced.

Imagine the unusual scenario in which an employee has a history of verbal or physical abuse. The employee may be somebody you just don't trust. Maybe he stands 6'7", weighs 300 pounds, and his physical presence alone is intimidating. Maybe the mere thought of being alone in the same room with this person is scary.

Fear is a peculiar thing. When people talk about fear, they treat it as a negative emotion that they should not feel. Experiencing fear does not make people feel good about themselves. Some people see fear as a weakness. There is a reason we feel fear, and understanding the purpose of fear assists in handling it. Generally speaking, fear helps keep us safe. Fear is an instinct that is similar to the need for food and sleep. Feelings of fear are a survival mechanism.

Think about the reason why you don't touch a hot stove. You fear getting burned and the pain that will follow. The same is true of hundreds of daily activities that we either do or don't do because we fear the consequences. For the most part, fear should not be ignored, but nor should it consume all of your actions and paralyze you. View fear as a warning signal, and use it to your advantage.

When dealing with an employee who makes you feel uncomfortable, take precautions to protect yourself and those around you. Then ensure that the encounter fulfills the objectives set forth for the meeting. Preplanning is a must. If the purpose of the meeting is to discuss performance-related issues, follow recommended procedures for counseling or disciplining employees. Before you inform the employee of the meeting, make sure that you have taken care of all of the preliminary details.

A conference room or other private room should be reserved to guarantee privacy. Before bringing the employee into the room, make sure that the room is suitable for the meeting. It should be reasonably neat and orderly. A box of facial tissue should be accessible in the event that the employee starts to cry. By having the tissue available, you eliminate the need for the employee to leave the room. Also have a pitcher or glass of water available for similar reasons.

Objects that could be used as weapons should be removed from the room or put away. Although almost any object could be used as a weapon, the room does not have to be completely barren. Scissors, letter openers, and paperweights should not be readily accessible. Remove the temptation by removing these objects.

If you think that the employee may become hostile or aggressive, do not inform him or her of the meeting in advance. Do not allow the employee to get personal belongings to take with them to the meeting. Women should not be allowed the opportunity to get their purses.

Give some thought to the best person to conduct the meeting. If a personality conflict exists between the supervisor and the employee, a manager or another person may be better suited to conduct the meeting. If the employee has a good relationship with and respect for another supervisor, consider having this person either conduct or attend the meeting. This person can also serve as a witness to the events that take place in the room.

Inviting a third party to attend the meeting is a good idea when the person conducting the meeting feels intimidated by the employee. Although the third party may not have an active role in the meeting, there is strength in numbers and the morale support of the third person may be enough to keep the situation under control.

If you are worried about the possible violent reaction of the employee, notify building security, if available. A security officer's presence can be as discreet or as obvious as the situation warrants. Consider expanding company policy to require a security presence during particular types of meetings.

Summon uniformed officers when you want their presence to be obvious. If a softer, more discreet presence is desired, use nonuniformed security officers. Officers in plain clothes may be less intimidating to the employee and offer the advantage of surprise if the situation sours.

Post the security officer within earshot just outside the room. An adjoining room may allow the security officer to hear the tone of the conversation without putting a glass to the door. An adjoining room also allows the security officer's presence to remain undetected.

The security officer should be trained on when and how to intervene appropriately in the meeting. Part of this decision should be up to the manager or supervisor who is conducting the meeting. His or her comfort level must be taken into consideration, as should the employee's typical behavior. The employee may have a history of becoming loud and boisterous without showing indications of violent behavior. A signal can be set up in advance to alert the security officer to enter.

The security officer can also be placed in the room during the meeting. This should only be done when a direct threat is perceived, unless company policy dictates otherwise. For some people, the presence of a security officer in the room makes them more defensive and more prone to aggressive behavior. If the security officer is stationed in the room during the meeting, he or she should not interfere in the meeting unless necessary. The employee being disciplined or terminated might try to bring the security officer into the conversation by asking, "Do you think that's fair?" or "Why are you here?" The security officer should not make comments or offer personal opinions.

Walk into the room before the employee and place a notebook or some other object in the chair closest to the door, forcing the employee to occupy another chair. This should be done as subtly as possible. An easy exit from the room is useful in case you need to leave or security personnel need to enter in a hurry. Think of the employee as a potential fire. You don't want that fire coming between you and the exit.

Maintain a comfortable distance between you and the employee. If you feel intimidated by the employee, a distance of at least four to six feet is ideal.

During the conversation, remain calm and in control. The employee may intentionally try to throw you off course or to gain control of the meeting. When the employee starts giving too much direction to the conversation, regain control with such comments as, "We're not here to talk about Joe." Keep the dialogue focused on the employee's performance and the actions needed to improve performance.

Pay attention to your body language. You want your body to send the same message as your mouth. Use your body language to reflect control and calm. Maintain direct eye contact with the employee. Don't look around the room or at others in the room. This could give the employee the impression that you are struggling to maintain control.

When sitting at a table, keep your hands on the table or by your sides, away from your face. Do not wave your arms in the air when trying to make a point. The employee may feel threatened or possibly even challenged. You want your actions to set an example for the employee. If the employee is already excited, you don't want to magnify that level of excitement with rapid body motions.

During the meeting, the employee may become agitated or irate. When this happens, your approach and mannerisms are especially important. The appropriate actions in this situation depend on the circumstances and your level of comfort with this individual.

It may be appropriate to continue the conversation at a later time, giving the employee an opportunity to cool down and think about matters. If you follow this course of action, tell the employee when you expect to resume the conversation. Do not set the meeting for more than a few hours or, at a maximum, a day later. Do not offer the employee this brief break if you believe that he or she might use this time to secure a weapon.

When you call a break in the meeting, do not lead the employee into believing that the matter is settled. If employees think that everything has been resolved, when they are called back to continue the discussion, they might think they are being disciplined twice for the same misconduct or mistake. This will seem unfair to them—and rightfully so.

If the employee becomes irate, attempt to calm him or her down before continuing the conversation or calling a break. Be a good listener. Whether you believe that an employee is right or not, he or she still has the right to voice an opinion. Some employees are able to calm themselves down if allowed the opportunity to vent their frustrations and concerns. This does not mean they have the right to be verbally or physically abusive to others. Control must still be maintained.

Allow the employee to talk about what he or she believes the problem to be and to offer a resolution. Allowing the employee to talk may bring out possible solutions. It may also uncover other problems that may be responsible for the employee's unacceptable behavior or performance. For example, perhaps the employee has been late and irritable every day for the past month because a family member is severely sick.

As the employee talks, be sensitive and empathetic to what is said. Try to understand the employee's perspective of the problem. The employee may be facing a personal problem of which you had no knowledge. Use your management and people skills to guide you through these situations. A common cliché is that people should leave their problems at home and not take them into work with them. To answer one cliché with another, this is much easier said than done. Managers and supervisors should not pretend to know the answers to the employee's problems, especially if they've never been faced with similar circumstances. Referral to an employee-assistance program or local not-for-profit counseling program might be the best answer. Everyone in supervisory positions should be able to provide quickly the name of a community agency that provides counseling services.

It may best serve the company to be lenient with employees when they are facing pressing personal problems that time will resolve. When the employee has a long, productive tenure with the company, the consideration you show will make this person even more dedicated than before after the personal problem is resolved.

The vast majority of cases involving irate employees do not end in a display of violent behavior. Do not overreact, and do not become overly paranoid.

As the employee talks, be positive and supportive. Simple nods will show the employee that he or she has your attention. Words like *yes* and *okay* are good to use to encourage a person who is upset. Do not agree with what the person is saying, however. Do not agree to statements that are not agreeable. Do not agree if the person says the company stinks, but instead use words to show that you are listening. Talking can go a long way toward helping a person cool down and become composed again. Use time to your advantage.

During the meeting, look for changes in behavior that indicate that the employee may be on the verge of becoming violent. The signs of potentially violent behavior are discussed in the next section.

SIGNS OF POTENTIALLY VIOLENT BEHAVIOR

Hostile customers or employees usually display warning signs that indicate that they are moving toward violence. By understanding these warning signs, you give yourself the opportunity to recognize the level of threat present and to prepare to protect yourself and others. Early recognition should allow you time to act to defuse the situation before violence erupts.

People act as they have acted before. The person with a history of violence against coworkers, family members, other people, or animals should be considered to have a propensity toward violence. This history should be viewed as a warning sign that the person is capable of producing violent behavior.

Agitation can display itself physically in the form of resistive tension, which is a physical response in the body that prepares a person for a fight. The blood supply to the muscles increases, for example. Chances are that the person will not even be aware of this reaction. Indications of resistive tension include the clenching of fists and a general tightening of muscles. In a sense, the person is flexing the body's muscles to warm them up.

Employees or customers may display excessive emotional attention along with exaggerated body movements. Key indicators of this are yelling, screaming, and possibly swearing. Their voices will get louder and louder, and they may begin to talk with their hands, wave their arms around, pound their fists on the table, or make rude gestures. They may kick and stomp their feet.

Employees or customers may go from this activity to a sudden cessation of all movement. They may become very quiet, almost calm, while they plan their next move. The next move may be a renewed attempt to talk rationally and to calm themselves down. They may suddenly have realized that their conduct is inappropriate and may attempt to regain composure. However, the cessation of movement could also be an indication that the person is finished discussing the matter. He or she may have decided that there is nothing you can say or do to help and that more talk is a waste of time.

Assessing Signs of Potentially Violent Behavior

- People who have been violent before may have a propensity toward violence.
- Agitation can display itself in the form of resistive tension.
- Many people clench their hands into fists, do shoulder shrugs, or get into a boxer stance before a physical encounter.
- The person may yell and scream, wave the hands in the air, or act in a similar manner.
- A person may switch from loud behavior to a total cessation of all movements.
- The person may look over your shoulders to see who else is present.
- Security officers should be called if you expect that a person might become violent.
- At the first sign of violence, call local law enforcement officials.

During the sudden quiet while the person is deciding on future action, maintain extreme caution. You don't know what the person is going to do next. If he or she has a history of violent behavior, you could be faced with a tough time ahead. Consider whether to summon security or other backup personnel to the scene. Because every situation is different, it is impossible to predict what actions are optimal at all times.

Immediately before a person becomes violent, he or she may display one or more of the following actions. When these signs are present, presume that the person is ready to become violent. Control the distance between you and the other person. Be prepared to use a bail-out route.

The person may take on what is referred to as a *boxer stance.* The legs will be shoulder-width apart, and one leg will be slightly ahead of the other, in a balanced position. The hands may be raised to shoulder or chest height. The person may start clenching the hands or positioning them in an offensive manner. The shoulders may shift or move back and forth as if the person were trying to stretch them out.

The person may quickly search the area behind you, looking for others who might come to your defense. People who are prone to fight are usually less willing to engage in a physical encounter if they know that others will be quick to respond.

As with any warning signs, at the first sign of violence, immediately notify the local police and building security if available. (See the box "Assessing Signs of Potentially Violent Behavior.")

8

Violent Behavior

Cathy's Story

Cathy was born and raised in the peaceful Midwest where, even though crime existed, it never significantly touched her life. In her early thirties, she was happily married to a serviceman and had young children. Like other wives of servicemen, Cathy packed up the family periodically and followed her husband from base to base. She worked outside the home, leaving her children at child care.

In other words, Cathy was a lot like other working women in the United States. On June 20, 1994, that changed. Cathy now has a story to tell that the rest of us never want to experience. She was the victim of workplace violence. She survived, but many others did not.

During our interview, Cathy's qualities were quick to surface. She is emotionally strong, intelligent, and brave and is surrounded with the love of family and friends. Cathy made it through the ordeal without severe emotional injuries. She was in many ways very lucky.

I'm relaying Cathy's story in the hope that others will realize the traumatic effects that violence can produce and will take whatever steps are necessary to prevent it. Violence can and does happen in every neighborhood, including the ones in which you work and live.

Cathy moved to the Spokane, Washington, area in the beginning of 1993. After settling in, she took a civilian job as a medical clerk in a mental health clinic located in the annex of the Fairchild Air Force Base Hospital. Cathy had worked there for about a year when tragedy struck. A former patient, Dean Mellberg, returned to the clinic and killed five people and wounded twenty-three others.

During the year that Cathy worked at the clinic before the incident, she scheduled appointments, filed paperwork, took dictation, and performed other clerical tasks. She never received any formal training on dealing with violent or hostile behavior. Looking back, she was never aware of any emergency plans for dealing with violence, but she was sure that the hospital had them. She thought the emergency room staff had probably been through training, as that was probably the site of the greatest danger.

The office where Cathy worked was across the parking lot from the main hospital. She worked on the first floor, where several doctors had offices. On June 20, just after three o'clock, Cathy sat at her desk, working on the computer.

The office was empty except for one other worker. The last appointment for the day was at three, and that patient was with the doctor. Cathy heard a loud bang and for a brief second thought it may have been a door slamming. Then she knew it wasn't the door. Cathy knew it was gunfire coming from the room next door, Dr. London's office.

Cathy ran around the office looking for a place to hide. She describes that moment as "running around the room like a chicken with its head cut off." There were two doors leading out of the office, but both of them led to the hallway where Dr. Brigham's and Dr. London's offices were located. Not knowing the location of the assailant, she decided to stay in the reception area.

Cathy's coworker slammed and locked the door when the gunman attempted to enter the office. The coworker broke through the screen on the window and jumped out of the room. Cathy hid under her desk, pulling her feet up so they couldn't be seen. She pulled her chair in behind her to make it appear that nobody could be under the desk. As she hid, the gunman walked by.

As Cathy hid under her desk, she thought of her husband raising their children alone. She wondered how he could raise them without her. She thought of her children growing up without a mother. She heard more shots coming from another office. She thought the shots came from Dr. Brigham's office, which was outside the other door of the office where Cathy was hiding.

Cathy knew that some employees had gathered outside the building to smoke. She heard a woman pleading with the gunman not to shoot her, then she heard more shots. Cathy wondered how many of the women were shot; sometimes up to six people were out there at a time.

An unidentified man frantically announced over the public address (PA) system that a gunman was loose in the building and that everybody should leave the hospital. Then he announced that the gunman was outside and that everybody should get back inside. Cathy knew by the shots fired at the pleading woman that the gunman was outside.

Cathy got to a telephone and called her husband. She told him that a gunman was loose in the building, killing people, then she said she had to go. She went back into hiding under her desk. She had no idea how many gunmen there were or why they were there. She thought they were terrorists, possibly from another country.

Chaos filled the offices. Cathy could hear people screaming, gunshots, and sirens. She didn't know if the police were firing back or if all of the shots came from the assailant. More frantic announcements came over the PA system. A "code blue" was called for the doctors who had been shot.

A man entered the lobby. For a moment, Cathy didn't know if he was the gunman or someone else. He was bleeding from a gunshot to his leg. When he said something like, "What is he doing?" Cathy knew that the man was not the assailant. Cathy wanted to help stop the man's bleeding. She tried to remember where the latex gloves were and then realized that they didn't have any in the office. She hid under the desk again, and the bleeding man hid under another desk.

A group of people broke into the office. They were medics and military police. They ordered everybody outside. Cathy went to Dr. Brigham's office and saw him on the floor. Even though the medics were all around and working on him, she could tell that he was dead.

Dr. London's patient was still in the office. Cathy took the patient and did what she was told to do—run. She and many others ran down the street, into the military housing area located off the base.

In the housing area, people were mowing their lawns and kids were playing outside. They hadn't a clue as to what was happening. Cathy yelled for everybody to get inside their houses.

Cathy was let into a nearby house to hide with perhaps four other people. From this house, Cathy called her parents and told them what was going on. The call was very short because nobody knew where the gunman was, and they had to hide.

Cathy recalls how strange it was to hear somebody knock on the door of the house. She remembers wondering whether somebody should answer the door. What if it was the gunman? Somebody did answer the door, and there were military police outside the house. The people hiding in the house were told to evacuate because the gunman was loose.

Again the people in the house began running down the street, toward the military base. Cathy remembers thinking that being in the street wasn't safe because they didn't know where the gunman was, but she ran anyway. She ran until she got inside the fence at the base. Then she stopped. People, lots of people, were there. They stood around, not knowing what to do next.

Sirens still filled the air, and they seemed to be coming from everywhere. Reporters with cameras were already there, and more were arriving. They had to stay on the other side of the fence, away from the people who ran to the base.

Cathy's husband found her at the base, and after a while they were allowed to leave. Cathy did not go directly home; she first stopped at the home of a coworker. From conversations with co-workers and others at the base, she found out that Dr. Brigham and Dr. London were both dead.

The next three days were filled with telephone calls from friends and family. Cathy's parents, who had left Spokane just days earlier, comforted and consoled her over the telephone. She told her story over and over. Everybody wanted to know all of the details. It wasn't until the day after the shooting that Cathy found out who the gunman was. She immediately recognized his name from the news reports. He was a former patient whom the doctors had recommended for discharge.

Cathy felt tremendous exhaustion in the days that followed. She attended a memorial for those who were killed on June 20. Even though she felt as if the doctors were members of her family, she did not attend either funeral because she wasn't sure she would make it through the services. Only a week earlier, they had all gone on a picnic together. Cathy's loss was tremendous.

Grief counselors were brought in for all employees, even those who were not there on the day of the shooting. At first, Cathy didn't want to go to the mandatory counseling sessions. After it was all over, though, she was glad she had. The friends and co-workers who were affected by the slayings banded together after the incident to form their own informal support group. They talked among themselves, consoled one another, and helped one another recover from the incident.

During the week that followed the shootings, the slightest noise in the night woke Cathy. She jumped out of bed and hid on the floor, afraid of the gunfire that she was sure had followed her.

Within days of the shooting, tragedy struck again. An air force plane crashed, killing the four people aboard. Cathy was sitting at home on the afternoon of the crash. The sounds of sirens again filled the air. Not knowing what had happened, Cathy went outside and saw smoke everywhere. Neighbors also went into their yards and into the streets. A neighbor said a plane had crashed. The second trauma only compounded the first.

A week later, Cathy returned to the office for the first time. She was terrified by the thought of entering the building where she had hidden under a desk to escape the gunman's bullets. When she entered the lobby, she saw, felt, and smelled a place different than what she had left.

The furniture was in disarray, moved out of the way and stacked on top of other pieces of furniture. The old blood-soaked carpet had been ripped out and replaced with new. The walls were in the process of being repainted. The doctors' offices had been stripped. Repair crews were still working to clean up the mess the assailant had left behind.

With the office in such disarray, there was very little work that Cathy could do. Patients were not seen. Every now and then she would have to pull a file for somebody, but for the most part, she stood around and talked to people who came by to pay their respects. Cathy felt frustrated at the fact that there was no work to do. She wondered why she was there. She felt that employees should not have had to go back until they were ready for them to work. The next day she stayed home.

Cathy and her husband decided to leave the area after the plane crash. They requested a humanitarian transfer, which was later granted. Cathy again packed up the family and followed her husband to a different base. The new base was within driving distance of her family.

This time, the move was different. The trauma she endured with friends and coworkers resulted in a unique bond between them. They had cared for and helped one another during a very difficult time. In some ways, Cathy felt like she was abandoning people she cared about. She was escaping the building and the base that served as a daily reminder of the events that happened on June 20.

When asked how the tragedy changed her, Cathy says that she now has a greater appreciation for the meaning of life. For now, she no longer works outside the home. Instead, she treasures the time she can spend with her children. Cathy is much more safety conscious than ever before. She doesn't trust other people the way she once did. She's more aware of her surroundings and the people around her and the children. For Cathy, the lesson learned from the shooting is that people should trust their instincts. When you sense that somebody or something is not safe, trust your feelings.

Cathy feels lucky to have survived the incident without permanent emotional damage. She believes that because she was emotionally healthy before the incident, received counseling afterward, and, most important, had friends and family to provide support, she has been able to leave the trauma behind her without too much difficulty.

FIGHT OR FLIGHT?

When violence erupts in the workplace, seconds count. When robbery is the cause of the violence, follow the recommended procedures in the next section for surviving a robbery. When the violence is caused by an estranged spouse, a current or former employee, a customer, or someone else, you need to protect yourself and as many other people as possible.

This is not the time to play hero. Most heroes are dead. This is the time to remain calm and to think rationally. If you are the target of the violence, do what the assailant says if doing so will help protect your safety.

Do try to escape if you can do so safely. If you are in the room with the assailant and are near an open doorway, you may try to escape if the assailant is distracted by another person. Do not be obvious. Be as quiet as possible. You do not want to bring attention to yourself or to your movements. If you are able to get out of the room, go to the safest place possible. Lock the doors, close the blinds or shades, and call the police. Thinking clearly in an emergency can be extremely difficult, but do try to stay as rational as possible. You may be the only person with the opportunity to call the police. Your coworkers and customers may be depending on you.

When you are in a room away from the assailant, lock the door and close the curtains if possible. If the room has a separate exit to the exterior of the building or away from the main center of violence, go. Gain as much distance as you can, and try to get into a protected area as quickly as possible. Do not maintain a straight line of vision with the assailant, you want to stay as hidden from view as possible. If you work in an office with many hallways and cubicles, turn down different hallways as you make your way to an exit or secure room. Call the police as soon as you are able to do so safety.

Do not try to confront the individual unless that is your only option. At a seminar dealing with workplace security and violence, a woman in the audience asked what to do if confronted by a person with a gun or a knife. I was shocked when the speaker advised participants to grab the weapon from the assailant's hands. The room erupted into a barrage of questions: How could a sixty-year-old woman without personal defense training unarm a young man with a semiautomatic rifle? How could someone take a knife away from a crazed person on drugs? How could an untrained person successfully take a gun away from an assailant who doesn't want to give it up?

The truth is, they typically can't. There are occasional stories about a receptionist who outwits a robber, but these stories are few and far between. Just as a person certified in first aid should not attempt to do heart bypass surgery, a person untrained in countermeasures should not attempt to unarm a person with a weapon. In most cases, the attempt would be suicidal. Even for people who have had training in this type of tactic, it should be a last resort. Ideally, once you give assailants what they want, they will leave. Only in a true life-or-death situation should you attempt heroic measures.

In some cases, trying to overpower the assailant is your only hope for your survival or the survival of someone else for whom you are willing to give up your life. If you know that by doing nothing you will be killed, you don't have much to lose by attempting to escape or fight. Run away if you can; fight only as a last resort.

Scott's Story

According to the U.S. Department of Labor's 1993 Census of Fatal Occupational Injuries, 1,063 people were murdered on the job in 1993. The vast majority of those killed (75 percent) were murdered during a robbery. This is the story of one of those victims, Scott Meyer. Scott's story is told by his parents, Norbert and Martha. The Meyers' only child was murdered on October 12, 1993, at eight o'clock in the evening during a robbery at the convenience store where he worked.

To understand the tragedy of Scott's murder, we must understand his parents. Norbert is successfully self-employed in contract construction. He has spent his entire life earning an honest living to support his family. He is a large man with a loud but gentle voice that sometimes quivers slightly when he talks about his son. Although he says that he doesn't mind talking about his son's murder, when given the opportunity, he'll change the subject. Right now, there's one matter that he talks about with intensity: reinstituting the death penalty.

Martha is a woman whom almost any child would be happy to call mom. She looks like the stereotypical grandmother who bakes cookies and does crafts in her spare time. She's retired from a job at a local hospital, where she had worked for many years. Martha is an intelligent woman who takes obvious pride in her home and family. Despite her grandmotherly appearance, she does not, and never will, have grandchildren. Instead, she finds company with her pet terrier.

The Meyers had thought about giving the terrier away to friends three months before Scott's death, but Scott convinced his parents to keep the dog. Martha believes that Scott's determination to keep the dog is now almost ironic because after Scott's death, the terrier played an important part in Martha's recovery.

Inside their historical, two-story house, pictures of Scott serve as silent reminders of the son they lost. A yellowed copy of their son's obituary hangs on the side of their refrigerator. Artwork created by Scott in his younger years is displayed with pride in the living room. A painting of the American flag and an eagle, which hangs over the fireplace, was a father-son project many years ago. The painting is a testimony to the family's belief in patriotism and freedom.

The Meyers describe their son as a responsible adult who was independent at the time of his death, yet lived at home with them. He led a quiet and private life. Scott never married and considered himself a "confirmed bachelor." He enjoyed activities with his parents as well as time spent with his friends.

Living in the neighborhood in which he was raised, Scott had plenty of friends who shared his hobbies. One hobby Scott really enjoyed was working on classic automobiles. He owned several cars and trucks that he enjoyed getting into show condition. He was a member of the local classic car club, where he showed his old pickup truck. After Scott's death, his parents were given an honorary membership in the club, and they continue to exhibit his truck at shows. The trophies awarded for the prize truck are displayed on a shelf in the living room.

Scott had worked at the same convenience store for seventeen of his thirty-four years. He had worked at other second jobs during his life, but he especially enjoyed working at the convenience store. The manager of the store and Scott had been close friends for a number of years, and they enjoyed a good working relationship. Scott also enjoyed talking with customers, many of whom he knew by name and had gone to school with.

Having been robbed twice before, Scott knew about the potential for violent crime in convenience stores. A year earlier, the manager had been shot during a robbery. The bullet grazed the top of his head but did not injure him seriously.

Scott's father describes the convenience store as "just a violent place." Over the years, Scott's parents tried to convince him to quit his job and find safer work. Scott typically replied that he wasn't afraid of the customers and that he enjoyed his job. According to his mother, his feelings may have started to change in the weeks before his death. On September 29, a local man was murdered on the job in a robbery at a laundry. No arrest was ever made in that case. Scott's parents believe that it could have been the same men who murdered their son, but there was not enough evidence for arrest.

After the murder at the laundry, Scott repeatedly told his friends and parents that he didn't believe he would ever see his thirty-fifth birthday and that perhaps it was time to move to another town. Scott's mother tried again to convince him to find safer employment. Instead, he reluctantly agreed to visit an attorney to have his will drawn up. He never did.

The Meyers describe the security in the store as almost non-existent. The store had two entrances: one facing the street and one in the back of the store. Because gas pumps were located on both sides of the store, the back door was locked only after nine in the evening. The store had no security cameras. Scott never mentioned to his parents receiving formal training on robbery prevention or what to do if a robbery occurred. In an interview with the press, the public relations director told reporters that employees are trained in robbery prevention and that a list of robbery prevention and survival tips is posted on the bathroom walls at all stores. The store had a floor safe, and company policy stated that whenever the attendant had $100 in cash, he or she was to drop the money in the safe. The store also had a policy that employees were not allowed to bring weapons into the store. A robbery alarm was located near the cash register.

A local county supervisor, Leon Mosley, visited the store almost nightly to socialize with Scott and the other clerks. Store security was a topic of conversation almost every night. Mosley was appalled by the lack of security provided for the employees. He described the store as a "violent tragedy waiting to happen." According to Mosley, after the sun went down, the store was frequented by customers with guns sticking out of their belts and pockets, and it was "a scary place to be." Because Mosley knew that employees were barred from bringing guns to work with them, he brought his own. After the murder, Mosley posted $1000 of his own money as a reward for information leading to the arrest and conviction of the murderers.

A month before his death, Scott had asked Mosley to help him find a different job. According to Mosley, Scott wanted to leave the convenience store where he had invested so many years of his life because of the constant threat of violence.

On the day he was murdered, Scott went to work as he had always done. Meanwhile, ex-convict Keith Taylor and another man, Reginald Nelson, roamed the city. Taylor was wanted by police for questioning in another murder in Saganaw, Michigan. A few miles away from the store, the two men kidnapped a woman who was parking her van in front of her house. They forced her into the back of her van and drove off with her. The kidnappers never injured her; apparently, they just wanted transportation to use during the robbery.

After driving around for a few minutes, the two men drove up to the back of the convenience store and entered through the back door. What happened in the store can only be pieced together by the evidence that remained. Moments after they entered the store, the woman in the back of the van heard a gunshot. She knew immediately that the men had shot the attendant. Court records indicate that Meyer had been beaten before being shot in the head at close range with a .357 Magnum. Medical experts believed that he died instantly.

The robbers left the store and got back into the van and started to drive. The woman felt certain that she too would be shot. After driving around, the men pulled into a parking lot at an apartment complex only blocks away. They got out of the van, leaving the woman in the back and the keys in the ignition. They told her to count to one hundred, and they fled. Moments later, when the men had not returned, the woman jumped into the driver's seat and sped away.

The Meyers were sitting at home that evening at 9:15 when the store manager's wife and a police officer knocked on their door.

The manager's wife told the Meyers that their son was dead. Moments later, Scott's best friend, Jeff, arrived. Jeff had heard on the radio that a male employee had been shot at the store, and he knew immediately that it had been Scott.

Jeff and Norbert Meyer drove to the store as friends and neighbors began arriving at the house. Norbert parked his truck in the parking lot and watched the police tape off the area and begin their work. He didn't need to go into the store. The manager's wife had already identified the body.

The murder occurred on Tuesday, and the two men were arrested on Thursday. The man later identified as the gunman, Reginald Nelson, was nineteen years old. The other man, Taylor, was twenty-six and had already served seven years on a previous robbery conviction. Nelson was convicted of kidnapping, robbery, and murder. He is serving a life sentence without the possibility of parole. Taylor is serving a sentence of forty-five to sixty years.

These days, Scott's parents are advocates of the death penalty. Norbert led a statewide campaign for reinstatement of the death penalty. Funded by a local businessman, the Iowans for the Death Penalty campaign was launched on the one-year anniversary of Scott's death. The bill was defeated by the Iowa Senate in February 1995. Norbert and Martha are very angry at lawmakers who they believe "care more for rights of the criminals than they care for the rights of the victims and their survivors." Decisions based on the cost to enact the death penalty and not the protection of citizens enrage the Meyers. They are already planning their campaign strategy for 1997.

The Meyers also favor legislation mandating security equipment and training for businesses that deal with cash and are open to the public late at night. Martha feels strongly about companies providing protection for their employees. She says, "Either protect your employees or close the businesses down at night." Norbert feels that all employees working in establishments susceptible to robberies should be warned of the risks involved with the job and trained on how to prevent and survive violence.

During the robbery, the sum of $73 was taken.

KEY ELEMENTS OF A ROBBERY

Before planning the actions to be taken during and after a robbery, it is important to understand the key elements of this type of crime. Employee education on the facts about robbery will displace misconceptions regarding this crime and will help employees act in a manner that does not put them or others in additional danger. Educate employees about the following:

- The fallacy of the "typical robber" stereotype
- Techniques and methods used by criminals in planning a robbery
- The robber's conduct during the crime

There is no such thing as a typical robber, and it is dangerous to assume that there is. Employees who expect a robber to fit a television stereotype are vulnerable to robbers who don't match their preconceived image. There are recorded cases of robbers ranging in age from eight to seventy-nine years old. There have been female robbers who committed robberies while carrying a small child. A robber can be any age, race, or gender.

The myths commonly associated with bank robberies include the following:

- Two or more bandits hold all employees and customers at gunpoint. This is probably the most common scenario played out in the movies. (Remember *Bonnie and Clyde?*)
- A lone bandit stands out from the business's usual customers by dress or appearance. The out-of-place bandit is easily identified the moment he walks into the building, allowing the bank teller plenty of time to activate the duress alarm.

The truth is that fewer than 20 percent of all bank robberies are of the mass holdup type, and it is usually impossible to identify potential robbers by their dress or appearance. The robber may be dressed in blue jeans and a sweatshirt or a suit and tie. He or she is usually not looking to attract attention.

During the late eighties and early nineties, there was an increase in a certain type of robber in Florida and California: the "crack robber." Crack robbers wear sunglasses and a baseball cap to hide their face from bank security cameras. Many legitimate customers often dress in this same manner.

Robberies result in the highest percentage of occupational fatalities in the United States. Convenience stores, liquor stores, hotels, and motels are a few of the businesses that are most susceptible to robbery. In 1993 it is estimated that a loss of $538 million was experienced nationally during a reported 659,757 robbery offenses. There were over 50,000 robberies in 1993 in convenience stores, gas stations, and service stations. The average dollar loss in a convenience store robbery was $449. In the same year there were nearly 12,000 bank robberies with an average dollar loss of $3,308.[1]

More typical is the late-night robbery by a sole bandit of a retail establishment. The bandit will often look for the business that offers the least amount of risk—an establishment that has a lone attendant, cash, and a limited number of customers or visibility from the street. Planning for the crime is typically minimal. The robber determines the easiest target with the most money and then waits for the opportunity to present itself. Sixty-two percent of all people arrested for robbery were under 25 years of age.[2] In many of these cases, less than $50 is taken.

Most people find it difficult to imagine risking their freedom for $50. To understand the high occurrence of robberies, we must understand the robber's perspective. To the robber, that $50 probably seems like all the money in the world; the robber believes that he or she needs that $50 much more than the store does. The robber might be looking for money to buy a drug fix.

More important than the monetary losses, however, is the potential physical or psychological injury to employees and customers. A business's paramount concern during a robbery should be the safety of all employees and customers.

What happens during a robbery? The average robbery lasts less than sixty seconds. In appearance, the robber looks like any other customer. The robber will single out one employee and will try not to gain the attention of other employees or customers. The robber may make demands either verbally or in writing. The robber usually demands all of the money in the cash drawer and may instruct the attendant not to use "bait money," or money that activates an alarm when removed from the cash register. The robbery will involve a threat of violence: A weapon was displayed in over 60% of the robberies reported in 1993. Guns were displayed in 42.4% of the robberies, knives or cutting instruments were used in 10%, and other weapons were used in 9.5%.[3]

ROBBERY DETERRENCE

Most bandits want to rob a single person and leave without attracting unnecessary attention. Their goal is to commit the crime, escape, and not be arrested. To accomplish this goal, the robber uses various criteria to select the target of the robbery. One of the physical elements that can encourage robberies is the layout of the lobby or cashier area. Minimum protection for employees and limited observation from the outside of the building work in the bandit's favor. The number and location of escape routes can aid the robber in fleeing the building. Robbers usually leave the building in an unhurried manner to avoid attracting the attention of other employees or customers.

Cashiers and receptionists who fail to pay attention to activities in their areas invite robbery attempts. Clerks who do not make direct eye contact with customers are also inviting to the criminal.

To deter robbery, employees should be aware of the total environment. A cashier who projects an image of alertness will help create an environment that is not favorable to the robber. Visible alertness is an effective deterrent for robbery.

Employees should greet each customer as he or she enters the lobby. Besides being an advantage for customer relations, this behavior helps deter robbers, who usually do not want to be seen before making their demands. Once the demand is made, the victim experiences fear and terror. These feelings, which are natural, prevent the victim from memorizing the robber's appearance. Instead, the victim concentrates on the robber's demands. Robbers know this and use it to their advantage. If the clerk or receptionist greets all customers and looks directly at them, he or she will be better able to identify the criminal later if a robbery does occur.

Receptionists should be trained to practice recalling descriptions of customers. They should be told to look for such factors as height and weight; hair, eye, and skin color; presence of tattoos or distinguishing marks; and clothing. After a little practice, they will begin to take mental notes of each customer's appearance.

Windows near the entrance where receptionists are located must be as clear as possible of all materials that block visibility from the outside. Obscured windows offer the robber the protection of not being seen from outside of the building. This reduces the robber's chances of being seen by witnesses.

Many office posters and announcements seem to find their way to the front door. Employees who put them there are not trained or educated in theft prevention. When you observe posters or other materials that block visibility on doors, contact the person who displayed them. Explain why the posters should not block visibility from the outside and ask that they be moved to another location. Most employees will gladly comply with this request when they know the reasons behind it.

SURVIVING A ROBBERY

Law enforcement officials recommend various procedures to decrease the risk of harm during a robbery and to increase the chances of apprehending and convicting the robber. Instruct employees to follow these ten guidelines during and after a robbery:

1. Avoid actions during a robbery that might increase the danger to yourself, other employees, or customers.
2. Activate the duress alarm system during a robbery only if you can do so safely.

3. Make a mental note of the robber's physical description.
4. Give the robber no more money than demanded.
5. Protect all evidence after the robbery.
6. Observe the method of escape if you can do so safely.
7. Notify local police after the robbery if they have not already arrived.
8. Control access into and out of the building.
9. List witnesses of the robbery.
10. Collect information concerning the robber's description and method of escape.

Responsibilities During a Robbery

During a robbery, all employees should do the following:

- Remain calm. This may be very difficult to do, but remember that if you panic, the robber may also. Your reasoned actions are needed to help protect your coworkers and customers.
- Cooperate. Listen and do exactly as you are told.
- Be courteous and polite.
- Don't try to talk the robber out of the robbery. The robber decided to commit the crime before entering the premises.
- Follow all instructions given, and do not argue with the robber.
- Tell the robber about possible surprises.
- Minimize movement; do not draw attention to yourself by making quick movements.
- Ask permission before taking any action. Inform the robber in advance of your actions. For example, say, "I am opening the drawer now" or "I'm getting my keys out of my pocket." Quick, unannounced actions will startle the robber and could lead to injury.
- When possible, keep any notes that the robber gives you. They may help police apprehend the robber and will also act as evidence later.
- Do not attempt to activate the duress alarm if it cannot be done without attracting the attention of the robber.

- Give the robber time to leave.
- Do not chase the robber after he or she has left the premises. Observe the escape route and obtain a vehicle description and license plate number if you can do so from inside the building.

Responsibilities After a Robbery

The moments following a robbery are filled with emotion and chaos. However, this is the time when direct and decisive actions are needed to regain control and activate post-robbery procedures. The actions taken in the first few minutes following a robbery can assist police officers with their investigation and may lead to the arrest and prosecution of the robbers.

Post-robbery responsibilities are divided into different categories: employee responsibilities, management responsibilities, and special assignments. The appointment of special assignment responsibilities should be determined before a robbery occurs to facilitate their completion and reduce confusion.

After a robbery, all employees have the following responsibilities:

- Do not discuss the holdup with others.
- Do not touch anything in the area of the robbery.
- Trigger the duress alarm if not already done.
- When possible without leaving the building, observe the robber's escape route and get a vehicle description and license plate number.
- Complete a physical description form.
- Be prepared to give a signed statement to police officers.
- Do not talk to the media.
- List the names and addresses of at least three to five customers who witnessed the robbery.

Management personnel have the following responsibilities:

- Remain calm as a role model for other employees.
- Escort any victims to a quiet room.
- Alert other employees of the situation.

- Ensure that the police are notified. Provide the following information:

    The building name and location

    Your name and title

    The time of the robbery

    A brief description of the robber and escape method

    Details of any injuries and whether an ambulance is needed

- Refer all press inquires to the designated individual.

After a robbery, the following special assignments must be completed by the predetermined employees.

Special Assignment 1

- Secure the reception or lobby area where the robbery took place. Block access to all areas that the robber entered, including the entrance, rest room, counters, couches in the waiting area, and magazine racks. Each business has a variety of places where a person can loiter before committing a robbery. The robber may have loitered directly outside the entrance before the robbery.
- Protect any physical evidence.
- Pass out physical description forms and pens to all employees and customers present during the holdup. Collect the forms as they are completed, ensuring that each form has the name of the employee or customer written legibly on it. Initial each form as it is collected. Give all completed forms to the police.

Special Assignment 2

- Lock all exterior doors.
- Station an employee at each entrance to direct emergency response personnel to the area, to allow only authorized people to enter, and to prevent employees and customers from leaving. If a customer insists on leaving, obtain his or her name, address, and telephone number.
- Report any unusual situations to the police.

The Duress Alarm

Robbers sometimes become agitated when they think that an employee has activated a duress alarm. For this reason, employees should not activate the alarm unless they can do so without attracting the robber's attention.

All employees who work near a duress alarm must be instructed on its exact location. It is not sufficient to point casually to the location of the alarm. If the location of the button requires employees to bend down or get on their knees to see it, ask them to do so. Do not let employees actually activate the alarm unless a test alarm has been arranged with the local police department or monitoring unit.

Employees must also be instructed on how the system works. Inform employees that the alarm is silent. They should not expect to hear anything when the alarm is activated. When they press the button, they should feel reasonably assured that the alarm has been activated, and they should not panic. Employees should be told if an annunciator panel is located elsewhere in the business.

Accidental Activation of the Duress Alarm

When an alarm has accidentally been activated, it is necessary to ensure that the proper officials are notified and that the alarm is reset. An employee who knows that he or she accidentally activated the alarm must immediately contact the designated person. If the false alarm occurs during the second or third shift, the supervisor or manager should be contacted immediately.

When notified of a false alarm, call the local police department immediately to advise that the alarm was an accident. Give your name and title and the location of your business. Remember that the police department will not know that the alarm was accidentally activated and will respond as if an actual robbery were taking place. When police respond to a duress alarm, they usually drive to the scene at high speeds. This response is necessary during an actual robbery, but when it is a false alarm it can present an unnecessary danger to the police officers and to civilians.

When a single location experiences several false alarms, police response typically diminishes due to the belief that all alarms at that location are false. This can be extremely dangerous to employees, customers, and responding emergency service personnel.

If the business is serviced by a central monitoring station, contact the agency to inform them that the alarm is false. Be prepared to give your account code number. The monitoring agency will contact the responding police department.

REFERENCE

1. U.S. Department of Justice, *Uniform Crime Reports: Crime in the United States* (Washington, D.C.: U.S. Government Printing Office, 4 November 1994), p. 27.

2. Ibid., p. 29.

3. Ibid., p. 28.

IV

After Workplace Violence Has Occurred

9

Managing the Crisis

POSTINCIDENT PLANNING

Recovery strategies should be in place before a violent event takes place. When a postincident plan is in place, detailed instructions will be readily available to employees and will allow for quick actions and decisions. During periods of high stress, such as those that occur after any type of disaster, it's difficult to think things through and make rational decisions. Thousands of details must be dealt with, and hundreds of decisions must be made.

When the decisions are made in advance and documented on paper, the recovery process is quicker and less painful for everyone involved. These prepared decisions sometimes save human anguish, and they sometimes save the company money and time.

The postincident recovery plan need not be extremely elaborate. Procedures and policies should be decided and written in advance. When determining recovery strategies, weigh the risk versus the cost. Recovery plans should include established time frames to expedite restoration. Vendor contracts and agreements should be included in the recovery plan, and vendor names and telephone numbers, including home telephone numbers, should be recorded. This will ease the burden later when you need to contact them.

In some cases, telephone lines and customer service inquiries must be transferred to another location until the business is ready to reopen. Other office locations may have to cover pending manufacturing orders if possible. It is important to maintain customer confidence during difficult times. Once customers start shopping elsewhere, it can be very difficult to regain their business.

After a violent incident, you will need to address security concerns immediately. Employees may no longer feel safe in their work environment, and they may want security controls to be tightened almost to penitentiary standards. It is not uncommon for employees to request metal detectors at every door, armed security officers, and bullet-proof glass in cashier or reception areas. Management must weigh the costs versus the benefits of such long-term security measures. The presence of additional security officers within the facility will help employees feel safe as they return to work.

It is important to plan for the physical cleanup of your facility before any emergency incidents. Imagine that a company experiences a fire with moderate smoke and water damage during the night. No matter what else happens or how much it costs, the building must be open for business at eight o'clock in the morning or the company will lose millions of dollars. Now imagine trying to negotiate a contract for the cleanup of smoke and water damage at three o'clock in the morning. The company's bargaining position is nonexistent, and the cleaning company knows this. The business will pay exorbitant sums to the first cleaning company that agrees to roll out of bed, if the business is lucky enough to find one!

Now imagine trying to convince a cleaning service to come in and clean up after a shooting incident involving injured employees. As Cathy described in Chapter 8, bullet holes, blood, broken furniture, glass, and other debris were everywhere. Companies

---

Business Recovery Planning

- For optimal results, recovery planning must occur before the incident.
- Once a violent incident occurs, it's too late to plan.
- Business recovery planning will lessen the impact on the business, the employees, and the community.
- Employees themselves will need time to recover from the trauma of the incident.
- Business recovery planning need not be extremely elaborate.
- Preestablished agreements with vendors should be included in the plan.
- The recovery plan should include telephone numbers for all employees, names and numbers for employees' family members, and vendor names and numbers.
- All personnel who are responsible for carrying out the recovery plan should have a copy of it. Copies should also be kept off-site.

---

that have not prepared in advance for cleanup had better get the big checkbook out if they are looking at vendor services.

Recovery from violence will be unlike recovery from fire or natural disasters. The employees, customers, and the community will need to recuperate from the trauma of losing control. They may also need to grieve for the loss of friends, family members, or coworkers. Asking employees to participate in the cleanup after a violent incident is asking too much and may hinder their personal recovery.

MEDIA COVERAGE

When a violent crime is committed, you can be certain that media people will show up. The media may be on the scene before all of the emergency response people arrive. Most newspapers and television stations have an employee designated to monitor police and fire radio channels. This notifies them of incidents almost as quickly as the local police and rescue teams. Many news agencies also have a toll-free number for citizens who know of worthy news stories to call in and report the story. Plan on the prompt arrival of reporters and television crews.

During the first moments following a bombing, shooting, hostage taking, or robbery, things will be chaotic. Not only must you ensure the safety of employees, obtain medical care for the injured, notify family members of the incident, and help police apprehend the assailant, you must also deal with countless questions from the media. Chances are they will be asking questions that you can't answer yet. Even if you want to provide details, you just don't know all of the facts immediately after the incident.

The media are a business just like most other businesses. Media representatives are there to do their job. Like many other businesses, the various media outlets are diverse. You may have heard horror stories about reporters who ruin crime scenes and broadcast erroneous stories in their rush to be the first to get the news. This is not always the case, but you must be able to respond to the potential damage reporters can cause. Having a carefully thought out and well-documented media coverage plan in place will facilitate better coordination with the press. Contrary to the beliefs of many, the media can be of tremendous assistance following a crisis.

An employee must be designated to handle all media contact. This person and a designated backup person should be identified in the response plan so there is no question to whom media inquiries should be referred. The media representative should be granted the authority to make statements to the media without prior approvals from higher up. Things happen fast, and a quick response is needed. Because this designated employee will represent the company to the community and possibly to a much larger audience, he or she should be skilled in public relations and speak-

---

Media Coverage

- After a violent incident has occurred, things will be extremely chaotic.
- Reporters will appear.
- Information in the first hours after the incident will, at best, be scarce and incomplete. You will not know the answers to all of the media's questions.
- An employee should be designated in advance to handle media contact.
- Other employees should be told in advance not to respond to media inquires.
- Full cooperation with the media should be attempted. The media can be of tremendous assistance in communicating with employees, customers, and the community.
- Rarely is a "no comment" statement in the best interests of the company. What the media (and employees) don't know they might make up.

---

ing. Forms can be designed to help coordinate facts and details to assist in the communication process.

Other employees should be instructed not to talk to the media immediately after a tragic incident. Most employees have not had much experience dealing with the media. They may try to accommodate media questions out of courtesy and the desire to help. However, they will not know all of the facts of the incident, and misinformed employees can easily, and unintentionally, provide statements based on hearsay or lies that will could cause unnecessary harm to coworkers, their families, and the company. As part of their training program, employees should be told in advance to whom they should refer reporters.

When dealing with the media, the company's spokesperson should provide only facts, not opinion. The spokesperson's opinion may not be that of the company or the other employees. Care must also be exercised not to make assumptions or provide details that might later be used in litigation. If the suspect is an employee or former employee, do not discuss particulars about his or her work history, especially on performance-related issues.

Most reporters will cooperate fully with the company's spokesperson. This being the case, the spokesperson should feel free to ask reporters to be patient in waiting for details. When reporters believe that the spokesperson is being up-front and honest with them, they will be more understanding of the needs of the company.

Rarely is a "no comment" statement in the best interests of the company. Reporters are there to get the story, and if the story does not come from the company's spokesperson, they will look elsewhere for their information. They might question employees, neighbors, and even patrons of the nearby bar and grill.

A press statement can be a good tool for informing employees of what is expected of them. Large businesses are usually not able to call every employee in a timely and effective manner. When the business is small, all employees should be notified by telephone.

The company spokesperson can help guarantee that employees are provided with factual information through press releases. Information on the business being closed, modified hours of service, or the movement of business operations to an alternate site can be passed along in this manner.

John's Story

In 1994, twenty-five-year-old John got the Christmas gift of a lifetime. Actually, it was the gift of life that John received. Like the cat that has multiple lives, John too began a second life. John spent Christmas Day in a hospital in New York heavily sedated as he recovered from numerous surgeries. The ordeal started on the evening of December 20 at approximately 8:20 during a robbery in the store where John worked.

A year earlier, John had been graduated from Slippery Rock University in Pennsylvania and was offered a position as assistant manager in a clothing store chain in Palmyra, New York. At a slim 6'3", John displayed youth and confidence. Life was good, and his future was full of promise.

John moved to New York and began working at the store. He reveled in his position, which offered an abundance of customer contacts. John loved people, and this was his opportunity to do what he loved best. He was proud of his ability to talk to even the rudest customers and have them walk away smiling. Going to work was a pleasure.

On December 20 at two o'clock in the afternoon, John began his ten-hour shift. The Christmas season was the busiest time for the store, and there were plenty of customers who needed attention. Later that evening, a man walked in and changed John's life forever.

As John was working, the man walked up to him and opened his long coat far enough for John to see at least two guns hidden underneath. The man demanded that John take him to the room where the safe was located. John described the robber as a very old-looking forty-five to fifty-year-old white man.

John did as he was told. He walked to the room and fumbled with his keys as he tried to open the locked door. After they went inside the room, the robber took out one of the guns and started hitting John in the face and head. The robber kept talking during the entire incident, saying things like, "I'm going to kill you." John was ordered to open the safe. As he tried to do this, the man kept beating him with the gun. John filled the gym bag with the day's receipts and did not offer any resistance. Store policy was to never resist during a robbery.

The man ordered John to take him to the door in the rear of the store. To do this, John had to walk back into the merchandise area of the store where approximately two hundred customers were shopping. During the walk to the back door, another employee called to John for assistance with a customer in the layaway department. John said he would be back in a minute to help. He didn't want to attract any attention that might endanger other employees or customers inside the store. During the entire time, the robber kept the gun tight against John's back.

Once outside the customers' view in the back of the store, the robber ordered John to run to the door. Again, John offered no resistance. At the back door, the robber pointed the gun, later found to be a nine-millimeter semiautomatic, at John's head. John remembers the man saying something like, "I told you before that I was going to kill you. Now I'm going to do it." The man hit John in the head with the gun again. The force of the blow forced John to close his eyes.

John heard a blast and immediately felt what he describes as the worst pain of his life. John doesn't remember if he lost consciousness or not, but he was suddenly on the floor. Blood was everywhere, and the robber was gone.

He tried to get up, but he was dazed and in severe pain. When he did stand up, the floor was slippery from his blood and he fell a second time. He got up again, and this time he made it through the door that separated him from the merchandise area of the store. He might have been talking or yelling at the time; he really can't remember.

He does remember the blood squirting and gurgling out of his chest. His blood had soaked his hair and was dripping into his face. He wondered if had been shot in the head. He wondered if he was going to die. He worried that the robber had reentered the store and had shot customers or other employees.

A nurse, who happened to be shopping in the store at the time, came running. She quickly started administering first aid while others called for the police and an ambulance. For John, the moments that followed are blurry. He may have faded in and out of consciousness in the store and in the ambulance. He remembers feeling total disbelief at what had happened.

At the hospital, three surgeons were immediately summoned: one to stop the bleeding in the severed blood veins leading from his chest to his brain, one to care for the nerves that had been injured, and one to try to reconstruct the bones that had been shattered in his chest.

The next day, a doctor encouraged John to call his parents in Iowa and let them know what had happened. John resisted, not wanting to worry his parents, especially before the holidays. At the doctor's prodding, John did make the call. He doesn't remember much of the call, only telling his parents that he had been shot in the chest. His parents arrived shortly afterward. John doesn't remember if it was before, after, or on Christmas Day.

Two weeks later, John was released from the hospital to begin the long process of trying to reclaim the sanctity of the life he had known only a few short weeks earlier. For John and for many victims of workplace violence, it proved impossible. The days of confidence and trust were gone.

The weeks and months that followed were filled with pain and despair. Friends and family tried to bridge the breach that now filled John's life, but John resisted. As with many crime victims, John suffered emotional injuries along with his physical injuries. John was robbed of more than the money in the safe that night. His poise and self-assurance were gone.

Physically unable to work, John spent the next four months finding solace in alcohol and self-destruction. He played "Russian roulette" with his motorcycle, unconsciously wishing for death. He no longer cared about the things he used to care about. He became abusive, and his relationship with his girlfriend deteriorated and eventually ended.

John suffered violent rages. He hit friends for the first time in his life. He no longer answered his telephone or returned calls. Executives from the company tried many times to make contact with the injured employee. Their calls were ignored. John left his home only for doctor's visits and to buy tequila and other liquor. John's religious beliefs were damaged.

This behavior continued for months before a nurse finally convinced John to see a counselor. Knowing the severity of his recent actions, John agreed. Based on his behavior and symptoms, the diagnosis was quick: John was suffering from severe depression and posttraumatic stress disorder.

Five months after the incident occurred, John started attending weekly counseling. It took another five months for John to start to feel that he had a future again. John was able to reconcile with his girlfriend, and they are now engaged to be married.

John still feels fear at the thought of walking down neighborhood streets. He still hates the thought of losing control of himself and the possibility of being victimized by another criminal.

The nine-millimeter bullet still sits in his shoulder. The nerve damage has not healed and his left arm is still numb, but John is starting to talk about going back to work again. During our interview, John made it perfectly clear that he believes that the clothing store chain where he was employed is a great company to work for and that the management seems to care about the employees. John is quite satisfied with the company, but for his next position, he is hoping for an office job that will take him away from the constant face-to-face customer contact that he truly enjoyed before.

POSTTRAUMATIC STRESS

Experiencing a traumatic event can have long-lasting and devastating psychological effects on victims of violent crime. The symptoms associated with the stress range from relatively mild to totally disabling, depending on a multitude of factors characteristic of both the victim and the circumstances involving the incident.

Before businesses can establish appropriate plans for intervention and therapy, they must understand the nature and causes of posttraumatic stress disorder (PTSD). Employee-assistance programs (EAPs) can be valuable to organizations that are developing business-recovery strategies. EAPs or other counseling programs can also provide tremendous assistance to employees after a violent or other traumatic incident in the workplace. With advance planning, the long-term damages of the incident can be managed so as to reduce the impact on the employees and the company.

During an interview in January 1995, clinical social worker Kenneth Wernimont shed some light on the disabling disorder that individuals may experience as a result of witnessing a traumatic event, such as a violent act or injury in the workplace. The disorder may also appear after other traumatic events that result in a person's feeling that his or her survival or that of a loved one is in jeopardy. For example, an automobile accident that kills or severely maims people and a tornado or other natural disaster that severely damages a person's livelihood are examples of nonviolent events that may trigger PTSD.

Posttraumatic stress disorder differs from temporary posttraumatic stress. When a person is still symptomatic a month after the incident, professional psychological help is needed for the victim to recover.

Wernimont has nearly twenty-five years' experience in clinical social work in the mental health field and has treated a number of patients affected by PTSD. He says that this type of diagnosis is relatively new to the field of mental health. Only a few years ago, a patient suffering from PTSD might have been given another diagnosis. The more accurate diagnosis of PTSD can be useful in identifying and treating victims who have witnessed or otherwise experienced a violent or traumatic event.

People who suffer from posttraumatic stress experience a variety of symptoms. They often experience recurring dreams about the incident. Although they may not relive the exact set of circumstances in the nightmare, the feelings experienced during the incident will be present. The emotions in the dreams may be symbolic of great levels of anxiety, fear, loss, and, in some circumstances, guilt.

The distress that the victims felt at the time of the incident commonly recurs. They may say that they are unable to shake an unpleasant feeling. For some, the recurring feelings may only surface when they come in contact with a stimulus that reminds them of the trauma. A prime example of this would be a person who had a car accident that killed members of his family. He may appear to be okay in most respects, but he may experience overwhelming distress whenever he attempts to drive a car. For other victims, the distress only occurs around the anniversary of the incident.

Flashbacks are another possible symptom of posttraumatic stress. This symptom is frequently documented among veterans. In a flashback, the victim actually acts and feels as if he or she is reliving the experience.

According to Wernimont, "the intensity of the reactions to traumatic events can in some ways, but not entirely, be predicted based on previous experiences." Wernimont postulates that patients suffering from PTSD may have faced other traumatic events earlier in life, possibly as a child or young adult. The patient often does not consciously make a correlation between the events. The victim who has had similar events earlier in life will be more severely traumatized.

"Society as a whole has taught individuals to suppress feelings," Wernimont says. "As a child we are taught to quit crying, hush up and not talk about dirty laundry." Later in life, peer pressure dictates the amount of tolerance individuals are afforded when recovering from stressful events. After the death of a loved one, there comes a time when friends, family, and coworkers tell the bereaved to get on with life. The grieving person is prompted to stop showing emotion. Unfortunately, in most cases, this is exactly what happens.

When the victim of a traumatic event fails to deal with its emotional impact, it becomes buried but it never goes away. The occurrence of a second event that produces a similar emotional impact can unleash the trauma concealed from the first event. As a result, the victim now has two tragedies to deal with.

Keeping emotions buried requires energy, resulting in less energy to focus on the more productive aspects of life. An increase in overall levels of anxiety, tension, and irritability is another by-product of trying to keep emotions hidden. The individual's overall well-being is diminished.

Wernimont believes that people can become so conditioned to covering up pain and suffering that they begin automatically to suppress distressing feelings without the aid of external forces.

"This is one of the reasons EAP services should be available immediately following a traumatic incident," he says. "The mental health professionals will allow the traumatized employees the opportunity to express their feelings as well as provide the tools needed to begin to process their feelings before they have the chance to bury them. EAPs will give the employees the information they need right away." Some people may even need to be granted permission to cry.

"The body has built-in defense and survival mechanisms, such as adrenaline surges, that allow an individual who is experiencing imminent, severe, and traumatic events to block the immediate feelings the body is experiencing," Wernimont says. "This reaction is common among those experiencing violent acts. This form of denial blocks the emotional impact of the trauma and allows the person to continue to function in the face of great trauma."

Feelings of detachment also can be symptomatic of posttraumatic disorder. Victims may lose interest in friends and family and become alienated from loved ones. They may isolate themselves emotionally. Employees who fail to recover from the trauma will seclude themselves from their coworkers, often eating alone and working in silence.

Victims may feel and live as if there is no tomorrow. Their plans become shortsighted, and their future may cease to exist. Employees who once talked a great deal about having children may forgo their plans. They may put career-advancement opportunities on hold. Long-term plans, such as obtaining a college degree or buying a house, may be laid by the wayside.

Addictive tendencies (such as addictions to alcohol, food, or shopping) can develop. These tendencies may be expressed in alcohol or drug abuse as well as a wide range of other obsessive-compulsive behaviors, such as eating disorders.

Posttraumatic denial is common and can be expressed in several forms. Victims may deny the incident ever took place. They may have amnesia regarding the entire incident or certain aspects of the incident. They may go to great lengths to avoid any stimuli associated with the incident. If the trauma was a car accident, for example, the victim may go far out of her way to avoid driving by the accident site. Traumatized employees might avoid the company cafeteria if the cafeteria was the location of the violence.

Victims who are seemingly able to deny the emotional impact of a traumatic incident are setting themselves at risk for the future. Just as the second event unleashes the impact of the first, these people are walking around with an emotional bomb inside them. It might be weeks, months, or even years later when they will encounter a stimulus that provokes the denied feelings to emerge.

Imagine for a moment that, unknown to you, a coworker is a victim of the classic date rape. She had dated the assailant once or twice before the rape, and she liked and trusted him. After the assault, rather than dealing with the emotional trauma, the victim, who mistakenly feels that she is partially to blame, suppresses her feelings in the form of denial.

After a while, she decides to date another man. At the end of the evening, he attempts to kiss her goodnight. She explodes, screaming, yelling, shaking, and crying. What the date didn't have any way of knowing was that he just provided her with a stimulus that exhumed her buried emotional trauma.

This type of situation can happen very innocently when dealing with employees on various other issues. Suppose that a subordinate of yours had a previous supervisor who degraded and humiliated him daily. When you try to instruct the employee, you may be the recipient of misdirected rage. In this situation, there are no winners. You lose, the employee loses, and the company loses.

An understanding of how the devastating posttraumatic stress disorder can affect victims of crime clarifies why immediate care is needed for workers who are traumatized in the course of their employment. The longer the employee is allowed to suppress his or her feelings, the longer the employee will require medical treatment later on. No responsible person wants to deny employees treatment and launch them into a life filled with pain and anguish.

Characteristics of Posttraumatic Stress Disorder

This disorder sometimes occurs after a person has experienced a traumatic event that causes severe distress. Events precipitating PTSD include a threat to the patient's life or another person's life, the destruction of the patient's home or community by a natural disaster or other event, and witnessing an accident or severe violence in which a person was killed or injured. The following list describes the characteristics associated with PTSD, where the duration of the effects is longer than one month.

I. The person with PTSD will reexperience the event in at least one of the following manners:
   A. Repeated distressing memories of the event
   B. Recurring distressing dreams of the event
   C. Sudden feelings of reliving the event, such as flashbacks, illusions, or hallucinations
   D. Recurring distress from events that symbolize the traumatic event, including the anniversary of the event

II. The person experiencing PTSD will avoid stimuli associated with the trauma by at least three of the following ways:
   A. Avoiding thoughts or feelings associated with the traumatic event
   B. Avoiding activities that might arouse recollections of the event
   C. Experiencing an inability to recall aspects of the event
   D. Viewing with decreased interest significant events in his or her life
   E. Experiencing feelings of detachment or estrangement from others
   F. Experiencing a restricted range of affect (i.e., a reduced ability to experience emotions)
   G. Experiencing the sense of a shortened future

III. The person experiencing PTSD will exhibit persistent symptoms of increased arousal characterized by at least two of the following:

A. Difficulty falling asleep or staying asleep
B. Outbursts of anger or irritability
C. Difficulty with concentration
D. Hypervigilance
E. Exaggerated startle response
F. Reactivity to events that symbolize or represent an aspect of the trauma

RESUMING OPERATIONS

There comes a time when the business must resume normal operations. The good of the company, its employees, the community, and the stockholders depends on the business again fulfilling the needs of its customers. "Business as usual" will never exist again. Those who have been affected by violence will never be the same again. Customers and people in the community may never view the business in the same manner again. Key people within the organization may be lost, and the company may need to find replacements for them. Management may falter and stumble as it tries to provide leadership and direction to the wounded company. Times will not be easy for a long time to come. Knowing this, expectations and goals can be modified to allow a gradual return to some form of normality.

With any type of recovery plan, the responsible individuals and their backups must be clearly identified. They must have the authority to make decisions without going through a sea of red tape for approvals. Things will happen quickly, and the decision makers must be able to respond quickly.

Typically, the owner, executive vice-president, chief executive officer, or other top official of the business is placed at the highest level of responsibility to ensure that the recovery plan is carried out. The managers of security, facilities, human resources, and public relations also have a share in the responsibility.

The security manager is responsible for ensuring security to the building and the employees. Immediately following an incident of violence, security services will be needed to control the crime scene until law enforcement officials take over. Security personnel will also be needed to assist with first aid and the coordination of emergency services. Witnesses will need to be located and taken to secure areas to wait for law enforcement officials to interview them.

After the incident, security services will most likely need to be bolstered. In the hours and days immediately following the violent act, additional security officers may be required to ensure that access-control measures are enforced. Reporters, sightseers, employees, their family members, and even neighborhood kids may try to gain access to the facility or the grounds. In general, do not provide access to anyone who does not need to be there.

After business operations resume, the presence of security services and additional security measures will be comforting to surviving employees. As employees return to work, they need to feel some level of security with their surroundings. They might also demand that extra security measures be established before they return to work.

The security manager will also need to investigate the incident. Additional security policies and procedures will likely be required, and the security and human resources managers must be able to respond to those needs quickly. The security audit should be reviewed to ensure compliance with other security issues.

The facilities manager coordinates the cleanup of the site. The services of the maintenance department or an external vendor will be needed to repair the building if damage was done. Bullet holes must be filled and painted. Any blood must be cleaned up. Consideration should be given in advance to selecting vendors with experience in blood-borne pathogen standards.

Broken windows and furniture must be removed or repaired. Carpeting may need to be replaced. As employees return to work, they should not be subjected to gruesome reminders of the incident. In one incident at a post office, the returning employees were shocked to see bullet holes that had not been repaired in the walls.

Human resources personnel have a vital role in the recovery process. Their actions immediately following the incident and in the days, weeks, and months ahead help determine whether the organization will survive. Employees are the company's biggest asset, and after a traumatic incident, extra care must be used to protect that asset.

An EAP service should be notified immediately after the danger has passed. If the company does not have an existing EAP, one should be selected as part of the prepared recovery plan. As a last resort, the telephone book will provide a list of consultant services that might be available at a moment's notice. When a disaster occurs, most people and businesses usually try to be accommodating, but preplanning is essential.

The human resources department can assist management in determining when to resume operations. The well-being of the employees and victims, their families, the community, and the business's customers must all be taken into consideration.

After incidents of workplace violence, some businesses never reopen. When the McDonald's in National City, California, experienced one of the worst cases of mass killing in the history of the United States, the restaurant was torn down, and a park was built in its place. McDonald's Corporation funded the construction.

Although time is said to heal all wounds, the wounds of the company will never heal if it stays closed too long. Consumer confidence will deteriorate if vital services are suspended for long. Like the old saying goes, the best time to jump on the horse is as soon as you fall off of it. Do not delay reopening the business for too long. You don't want customers to think that the business was permanently closed due to the episode. Consumer confidence must be regained for the benefit of your employees, customers, community, and stockholders.

V

The California Occupational Safety and Health Administration's Model Program

10

The California Occupational Safety and Health Administration Addresses Workplace Violence

A MODEL PROGRAM WORTH A LOOK

In August 1994, the California Occupational Safety and Health Administration (CAL/OSHA) published a set of safety guidelines designed to prevent workplace violence. These guidelines were published after it became apparent that workplace violence was a very serious threat to the safety and well-being of employees in the state. The guidelines encompass a range of security concerns, from robbery prevention to self-audit procedures.

Development of the guidelines began at a conference on workplace security in Los Angeles in April 1994. An advisory committee was formed to examine the issue of workplace violence in

California and to explore techniques for preventing it. During the April conference, "many advisory committee participants commented that the idea of developing a standard specific to workplace security and emergency action plans should be actively explored."[1]

Since then, CAL/OSHA has drafted a model Injury and Illness Prevention Program for Workplace Security (reproduced at the end of this chapter). The model program is unique for a couple of reasons. First, it brings together the fields of safety and security. The Occupational Health and Safety Administration (OSHA) offices, including CAL/OSHA, have typically addressed safety issues in the workplace, but not security. Although OSHA has had the legal authority to issue citations for security issues that constitute a hazard for employees under its General Duty Clause, it usually focuses on health and safety hazards resulting from hazardous work.

Another interesting aspect of the program is that businesses in California are not currently required by CAL/OSHA regulations to follow the model program. A footer is included on every page of the model program advising readers that compliance is not required, but that when hazards do exist, the reader may want to use all or parts of the model.

This statement is, in ways, deceiving. Business owners who ignore the recommendations because they believe that the model program does not pertain to them need to reconsider. OSHA's General Duty Clause states that employers must provide their employees with a safe work environment, free of known hazards. When a business recognizes that a safety hazard does exist and fails to correct that hazard, it could be cited under the General Duty Clause. OSHA recognizes the risks associated with violent crimes as safety hazards. In addition, OSHA's regulations are only a small part of the regulatory environment surrounding security issues. Failure to amend a recognized hazard could prove costly if a lawsuit is filed charging the employer with negligence. So, although OSHA may not specifically require businesses to comply with its security standards, the business owner and other responsible indi-

Table 10–1 Work-related deaths in California.

	1993		1992	
Cause of Death	*Number*	*Percentage*	*Number*	*Percentage*
Assaults and violent acts	230	37.4	193	30.0
Transportation accidents	226	36.7	253	39.3
All other[a]	158	25.7	196	30.4
Total[b]	615	100	644	100

Source: CAL/OSHA Guidelines for Workplace Security (San Francisco: Department of Industrial Relations, Division of Occupational Safety and Health, August 1994).

[a]This category includes contact with objects and equipment, falls, exposure to harmful substances or environments, and fires and explosions.

[b]Totals may include data for subcategories not shown separately.

viduals may be legally responsible for failing to maintain a safe and healthy work environment.

Looking at the statistics presented, it's easy to see why concern prompted CAL/OSHA to act. According to the California Division of Labor Statistics and Research, there were 615 work-related deaths in the state in 1993. Of the 615 recorded deaths, 230 (37.4 percent) were directly related to assaults and other violent acts, a dramatic increase from 1992. In 1993, violence in the workplace was the leading cause of work-related deaths in California. Table 10–1 illustrates the role of violence in work-related deaths in California.

The cause of death for the majority of women killed on the job in 1993 was homicide. In that year, 48.2 percent of the women who died on the job were murdered. They were killed by robbers, estranged partners, former employees, and customers. Women were more likely to die on the job in an act of violence than from almost all other causes put together.

When we think about the friends and families who are left to mourn these victims' deaths, it's easy to understand the urgency in developing guidelines to prevent occupational violence. Although no one likes to have his or her actions regulated by the government, it should be evident that some kind of action plan is needed to stop the bloodshed.

THINGS TO COME

Just as California's antistalking laws started a movement that swept across the country, CAL/OSHA's model workplace security program will likely become part of a national law affecting businesses across the United States. Security and safety managers who want to act now to ensure compliance later should look to the CAL/OSHA model program for insight into what the future might hold.

There is ample reason to believe that CAL/OSHA's model program will become increasingly significant to businesses all across the United States in the years to come. Laws exist today to regulate such trivia as the thickness of pickles served in fast-food restaurants. Compare the significance of pickle thickness to that of workplace violence and other crimes prevalent in today's society. How long will it be before federal laws mandate that all businesses address security issues?

The following is a reproduction of the *CAL/OSHA Model Injury and Illness Prevention Program for Workplace Security.*

CAL/OSHA INJURY AND ILLNESS PREVENTION PROGRAM FOR WORKPLACE SECURITY, SEVENTH DRAFT, JANUARY 24, 1995

Who should use this program? No one is required to use this program. However, if you determine that workplace security hazards exist in your workplace, you may want to use some, or all, of this model program or develop your own program independently.

Many workplaces are at risk for workplace violence, but certain workplaces are recognized to be at significantly higher risk than others. Therefore every employer should perform an initial assessment to identify workplace security issues. If the initial assessment determines that employees are at significant risk for workplace violence then the employer should review the material presented in this model program.

There are a number of risk factors that have been shown to contribute to the risk of workplace violence. If you have one or more of the following factors at your workplace then you should consider your workplace to be at potential risk of violence.

- Exchange of money.
- Working alone at night and during early morning hours.
- Availability of valued items (e.g.: money and jewelry).
- Guarding money or valuable property or possessions.
- Performing public safety functions in the community.
- Working with patients, clients or customers known or suspected to have a history of violence.
- Having employees with a history of assaults or who exhibit belligerent, intimidating and threatening behavior to others.

These are just some of the major factors that contribute to workplace violence. If you have identified any of these, or other indicators of violence, in the workplace then a further evaluation should be performed.

Workplace Violence in California

The circumstances associated with workplace violence in California can be divided into three major types. However, it is important to keep in mind that a particular occupation or workplace may be subject to more than one type.

Type I

In California, the majority of workplace homicides involve a person entering a small late night retail establishment, e.g., liquor store, gas station or convenience store, to commit a robbery. During the commission of the robbery, an employee or, more likely, the proprietor is killed or injured.

Employees or proprietors who have face-to-face contact and exchange money with the public, who work late at night and into the early morning hours, and who work alone or in very small numbers are at greatest risk of a Type I event. While the assailant may feign being a customer as a pretext to enter the establishment, he or she has no legitimate relationship to the workplace.

Retail robberies resulting in workplace assaults usually occur between the hours of seven in the evening and two in the morning and are most often armed robberies. In addition to employees who are classified as cashiers, many victims of late night retail violence are supervisors or proprietors who are attacked while locking up their establishment for the night or janitors who are assaulted while cleaning the establishment after it is closed.

Other occupations/workplaces may be at risk of a Type I event. For instance, assaults on taxicab drivers also involve a pattern similar to retail robberies. The attack is likely to involve an assailant pretending to be a bona fide passenger during late night or early morning hours who enters the taxicab to rob the driver of his or her fare receipts. Type I events also involve security guards. It has been known for some time that security guards are at risk of assault when protecting valuable property that is the object of an armed robbery.

Type II

A Type II workplace violence event involves an assault by someone who is either the recipient or the object of a service provided by the affected workplace or the victim.

Type II events involve victims who provide services to the public. These events chiefly involve assaults on public safety and correctional personnel, municipal bus or rail drivers, health care and social service providers, sales personnel, and other public or private service sector employees who provide professional, public safety, administrative or business services to the public.

Law enforcement personnel are at risk of assault from the object of public safety services when making arrests, conducting drug raids, responding to calls involving robberies or domestic disputes, serving warrants and eviction notices and investigating suspicious vehicles. Similarly, correctional personnel are at risk of assault while guarding and transporting jail or prison inmates.

Of increasing concern, though, are Type II events involving assaults to the following types of service providers:

1. Medical care providers in acute care hospitals, long-term care facilities, outpatient clinics and home health agencies;
2. Mental health and psychiatric care providers in inpatient facilities, outpatient clinics, residential sites and home health agencies;
3. Alcohol and drug treatment providers;
4. Social welfare providers in unemployment offices, welfare eligibility offices, homeless shelters, probation offices and child welfare agencies; and
5. Other types of service providers, e.g., justice system personnel, customer service representatives and delivery personnel.

Unlike Type I events, which often represent irregular occurrences in the life of any particular at-risk establishment, Type II events occur on a daily basis in many service establishments and therefore represent a more pervasive risk for certain service providers.

Type III
The Type III workplace violence event consists of an assault by an individual who has some employment-related involvement with the workplace. The Type III event usually involves a threat of physical action by a current or former employee, supervisor or manager; by a current or former spouse or lover; a relative or friend; or some other person who has a dispute involving an employee of the workplace.

Available data indicates that a Type III event is not associated with a specific type of workplace or occupation. Any workplace can be at risk of a Type III event. However, Type III events account for a much smaller proportion of fatal workplace injuries than Type I and II. Type III fatalities often attract significant media attention and are perceived as much more common than they actually are.

The Model Program

Our establishment's Injury and Illness Prevention (IIP) Program for Workplace Security addresses the hazards known to be associated with the three major types of workplace violence. Type I workplace violence involves a violent act by an assailant with no legitimate relationship to the workplace, who enters the workplace to commit a robbery or other criminal act. Type II involves a violent act by a recipient of a service provided by our establishment, such as a client, patient, customer, passenger or a criminal suspect or prisoner. Type III involves a violent act by a current/former employee, supervisor or manager, or other person who has some employment-related involvement with our establishment, such as an employee's spouse or lover, an employee's relative or friend, or other person who has a dispute with one of our employees.

Responsibility

We decided to assign responsibility for security in our workplace. The IIP Program administrator for workplace security is our safety manger, who has authority and responsibility for implementing the provisions of this program for our company. All managers and supervisors are responsible for implementing and maintaining this program in their work areas and for answering employee questions about the program.

Compliance

We have established the following policy to ensure compliance with our workplace rules on workplace security. Management of our facility is committed to ensuring that all safety and health policies and procedures involving workplace security are clearly communicated and understood by all employees.

All employees are responsible for using safe workplace practices, for following all directives, policies and procedures, and for assisting in maintaining a safe and secure work environment.

Our system of ensuring that all employees, including managers and supervisors, comply with safe work practices that are designed to make the workplace more secure, and do not engage in threats or physical actions which create a security hazard for others in the workplace, include:

1. Informing employees, supervisors, and managers of the provisions of our IIP Program for workplace security.
2. Evaluating the performance of all employees in complying with our company's workplace security measures.
3. Recognizing employees who perform work practices which promote security in the workplace.
4. Providing training and/or counseling to employees whose performance in complying with work practices designed to ensure workplace security is deficient.
5. Disciplining workers for failure to comply with workplace security practices.
6. The following practices that ensure employee compliance with workplace security directives, policies and procedures.

Communication

At our establishment, we recognize that to maintain a safe, healthy and secure workplace, we must have open, two-way communication between all employees, including managers and supervisors, on all workplace and security issues. Our company has a communication system designed to encourage continuous flow of safety, health and security information between management and our employees without fear of reprisal and in a way that is readily understandable. Our communication system consists of the checked items:

- ☐ New employee orientation on our establishment's workplace security policies, procedures, and work practices.
- ☐ Periodic review of our workplace security with all personnel.
- ☐ Training programs designed to address specific aspects of workplace security unique to our establishment.
- ☐ Regularly scheduled safety meetings with all employees to discuss workplace security.

☐ Translation into language readily understandable by all personnel.

☐ Posted or distributed workplace security information.

☐ A system for workers to inform management about workplace hazards or threats of violence.

☐ Procedures for protecting employees who report threats from retaliation by the person who makes the threat.

☐ A labor/management/safety and health committee that meets regularly, prepares written records of the safety and health committee meetings, reviews results of the periodic scheduled workplace security inspections, reviews incidents of workplace violence and makes suggestions to management for the prevention of future incidents, reviews threats and incidents, and submits recommendations to assist in the evaluation, training, and counseling of employees.

☐ Our establishment has less than ten employees and communicates with and instructs employees orally about general safe work practices with respect to workplace security.

☐ Other:

Hazard Assessment

We will be performing workplace hazard assessment for workplace security in the form of periodic inspections. Periodic inspections to identify and evaluate workplace security hazards and threats of workplace violence are performed by the following observer(s) in the following areas of our workplace:

Observer Area

Periodic inspections are performed according to the following schedule:

1. Frequency (daily, weekly, monthly, etc.);
2. When we initially establish our IIP Program for workplace security;
3. When new, previously unidentified security hazards are recognized;

4. When occupational injuries or threats of injuries occur; and
5. Whenever workplace security conditions warrant an inspection.

Periodic inspections for security hazards consist of identification and evaluation of workplace security hazards and changes in employee work practices and may require assessing for more than one type of workplace violence. Our establishment performs inspections for each type of workplace violence by using methods specified below to evaluate workplace security hazards.

Inspections for Type I workplace security hazards include assessing:

1. The exterior and interior of the workplace for its attractiveness to robbers.
2. The need for security surveillance measures, such as mirrors and cameras.
3. Posting of signs notifying the public that limited cash is kept on the premises.
4. Procedures for employees responding during a robbery or other criminal act.
5. Procedures for reporting suspicious persons or activities.
6. Posting of emergency telephone numbers for law enforcement, fire and medical services where employees have access to a telephone with an outside line.
7. Limiting of the amount of cash on hand and using time access safes for large bills.
8. Other:

Inspections for Type II workplace security hazards include assessing:

1. Access to, and freedom of movement within, the workplace.
2. Adequacy of workplace security systems, such as door locks, security windows, physical barriers and restraint systems.
3. Frequency and severity of threatening or hostile situations that may lead to violent acts by persons who are service recipients of our establishment.

4. Employees' skill in safely handling threatening or hostile service recipients.
5. Effectiveness of systems to warn others of a security danger or to summon assistance, e.g., alarms or panic buttons.
6. The use of work practices such as "buddy" systems for specified emergency events.
7. The availability of employee escape routes.
8. Other:

Inspections for Type III workplace security hazards include assessing:

1. How effectively our establishment's antiviolence policy has been made known to employees, supervisors or managers.
2. How effectively our establishment's management and employees relate to each other.
3. Awareness by employees, supervisors and managers of the warning signs of potential workplace violence.
4. Access to, and freedom of movement within, the workplace by nonemployees, including recently discharged employees or persons with whom one of our employees is having a dispute.
5. Frequency and severity of employee reports of threats of physical or verbal abuse by managers, supervisors or other employees.
6. Any prior violent acts, threats of physical violence, verbal abuse, property damage or other signs of strain or pressure in the workplace.
7. Employee disciplinary and discharge procedures.
8. Other:

Incident Investigations

We have established the following policy for investigating incidents of workplace violence. Our procedures for investigating incidents of workplace violence, which includes threats and physical injury, include:

1. Reviewing all previous incidents;
2. Visiting the scene of an incident as soon as possible;
3. Interviewing threatened or injured employees and witnesses;
4. Examining the workplace for security risk factors associated with the incident, including any previous reports of inappropriate behavior by the perpetrator;
5. Determining the cause of the incident;
6. Taking corrective action to prevent the incident from recurring;
7. Recording the findings and corrective actions taken; and
8. Other:

Hazard Correction

Hazards which threaten the security of employees shall be corrected in a timely manner based on severity when they are first observed or discovered.

Corrective measures for Type I workplace security hazards include:

1. Making the workplace unattractive to robbers.
2. Utilizing surveillance measures, such as cameras or mirrors, to provide information as to what is going on outside and inside the workplace.
3. Procedures for reporting suspicious persons or activities.
4. Posting of emergency telephone numbers for law enforcement, fire and medical services where employees have access to a telephone with an outside line.
5. Posting of signs notifying the public that limited cash is kept on the premises.
6. Limiting the amount of cash on hand and using time access safes for large bills.
7. Employee, supervisor and management training on emergency action procedures.
8. Other:

Corrective measures for Type II workplace security hazards include:

1. Controlling access to, and freedom of movement within, the workplace consistent with business necessity.
2. Ensuring the adequacy of workplace security systems, such as door locks, security windows, physical barriers and restraint systems.
3. Providing employee training in recognizing and handling threatening or hostile situations that may lead to violent acts by persons who are service recipients of our establishment.
4. Placing effective systems to warn others of a security danger or to summon assistance, e.g., alarms or panic buttons.
5. Providing procedures for a "buddy" system for specified emergency events.
6. Ensuring adequate employee escape routes.
7. Other:

Corrective measures for Type III workplace security hazards include:

1. Effectively communicating our establishment's antiviolence policy to all employees, supervisors and managers.
2. Improving how effectively our establishment's management and employees relate to each other.
3. Increasing awareness by employees, supervisors and managers of the warning signs of potential workplace violence.
4. Controlling access to, and freedom of movement within, the workplace by nonemployees, including recently discharged employees or persons with whom one of our employees is having a dispute.
5. Providing counseling to employees, supervisors or managers who exhibit behavior that represents strain or pressure which may lead to physical or verbal abuse of coworkers.
6. Ensuring that all reports of violent acts, threats of physical violence, verbal abuse, property damage or other signs of strain or pressure in the workplace are handled effectively by management and that the person making the report is not subject to retaliation by the person making the threat.

7. Ensuring that employee disciplinary and discharge procedures address the potential for workplace violence.
8. Other:

Training and Instruction

We have established the following policy on training all employees with respect to workplace security. All employees, including managers and supervisors, shall have training and instruction on general and job-specific workplace security practices. Training and instruction shall be provided when the IIP Program for Workplace Security is first established and then periodically thereafter. Training shall also be provided to all new employees and all other employees for which training has not previously been provided and to all employees, supervisors and managers given new job assignments for which specific workplace security training for that job assignment has not previously been provided. Additional training and instruction will be provided to all personnel affected whenever the employer is made aware of a new or previously unrecognized security hazard.

General workplace security training and instruction includes, but is not limited to, the following:

1. Explanation of the IIP Program for Workplace Security, including measures for reporting any violent acts, threats of violence or verbal abuse;
2. Recognition of workplace security hazards, including the risk factors associated with the three types of workplace violence;
3. Measures to prevent workplace violence, including procedures for reporting workplace security hazards or threats to managers and supervisors;
4. Ways to defuse hostile or threatening situations;
5. Measures to summon others for assistance;
6. Employee routes of escape;
7. Notification of law enforcement authorities when a criminal act may have occurred;
8. Emergency medical care provided in the event of any violent act upon an employee; and

9. Post-event trauma counseling for those employees desiring such assistance.

In addition, we provide specific instructions to all employees regarding workplace security hazards unique to their job assignment, to the extent that such information was not already covered in other training.

We have chosen the following checked items for Type I training and instruction for managers, supervisors and employees:

☐ Crime awareness.
☐ Location and operation of alarm systems.
☐ Communication procedures.
☐ Proper work practices for specific workplace activities or assignments, such as late night retail salesperson, taxi-cab driver, or security guard.
☐ Other:

We have chosen the following checked items for Type II training and instruction for managers, supervisors and employees:

☐ Self-protection.
☐ Dealing with angry, hostile and threatening individuals.
☐ Location, operation, care, and maintenance of alarm systems and other protective devices.
☐ Communication procedures.
☐ Determination of when to use the "buddy" system or other assistance from coworkers.
☐ Awareness of indicators that lead to violent acts by recipients of service providers.
☐ Other:

We have chosen the following checked items for Type III training and instruction for managers, supervisors and employees:

☐ Preemployment screening practices.
☐ Employee-assistance programs.
☐ Awareness of indicators that lead to violent acts.

☐ Managing with respect and consideration for employee well-being.
☐ Review of antiviolence policy and procedures.
☐ Other:

Record Keeping
We have checked one of the following categories as our policy.

Category 1
Our establishment has twenty or more workers; has a workers' compensation modification rate of greater than 1.1 and is not on a designated low hazard industry list; or is on a designated high hazard industry list. We have taken the following steps to implement and maintain our IIP Program:

1. Records of workplace security, the person or persons conducting the inspection, the unsafe conditions and work practices that have been identified and the action taken to correct the identified unsafe conditions and work practices are recorded on a hazard assessment and correction form; and
2. Documentation of safety, health and security training for each worker, including the worker's name or other identifier, training dates, type(s) of training, and training providers are recorded on a worker training and instruction form.

Inspection records and training documentation will be maintained according to the following checked schedule:

☐ For three years, except for training records of employees who have worked for less than one year, which are provided to the worker upon termination of employment; or
☐ Since we have less than ten workers, including managers and supervisors, we only maintain inspection records until the hazard is corrected and only maintain a log of instructions to workers with respect to worker job assignments when they are first hired or assigned new duties.

Category 2

Our establishment has fewer than twenty workers and is not on a designated high hazard industry list. We are also on a designated low hazard industry list or have a workers' compensation experience modification rate of 1.1 or less and have taken the following steps to implement and maintain our IIP Program:

1. Records of hazard assessment inspection; and
2. Documentation of safety, health and security training for each worker.

   Inspection records and training documentation will be maintained according to the following checked schedule:

☐ For three years, except for training records of employees who have worked for less than one year, which are provided to the employee upon termination of employment; or

☐ Since we have less than ten workers, including managers and supervisors, we maintain inspection records only until the hazard is corrected and only maintain a log of instructions to workers with respect to worker job assignments when they are first hired or assigned new duties.

Category 3

We are a local governmental entity (any county, city, or district, and any public or quasi-public corporation or public agency therein), and we are not required to keep written records of the steps taken to implement and maintain our IIP Program.[2]

REFERENCES

1. *CAL/OSHA Guidelines for Workplace Security* (San Francisco: Department of Industrial Relations, Division of Occupational Safety and Health, August 1994), p. 21.
2. *CAL/OSHA Model Injury and Illness Prevention Program for Workplace Security* (San Francisco: Department of Industrial Relations, Division of Occupational Safety and Health, January 24, 1995).

Conclusion

The nineties will go down in business history as the decade in which managers became leaders and departments became teams. The team-management philosophy will take U.S. companies into a new era of productivity and effectiveness. Businesses that don't make this change will fall to the wayside.

By establishing teams in the workplace to address and deal with workplace violence, we can stop it. We all have a responsibility to ourselves, to our coworkers, and to our employers to work together to prevent the unnecessary loss of live. In this sense, all of us are on the same team.

To some people, workplace violence seems very remote. They don't believe that violence will strike their company or harm a family member or friend, but it can, and it does, every day. Without the prevention, intervention, and resolution of key issues, the violence will continue. Pointing fingers, placing blame, and ignoring the issues only feeds the vicious cycle.

Workplace violence is preventable. In almost every case of workplace violence, there was a point in time when something could have been done to prevent the bloodshed. Many of the measures used to decrease workplace violence are preventive by nature. Policies, procedures, training, and employment screenings are only a few of the tools that companies can use to prevent violence.

This is your call to action. This book covered many procedures that will help decrease or stop workplace violence. Reading about them is not enough, though. You must take action. You have been handed the knowledge you need. Now it's up to you to use it to make a difference.

Index

Abnormal behavior
   causes of, 13
   normal versus, 11–14
Absenteeism
   alcohol abuse and, 23, 50
   domestic violence and, 32, 34
   drug abuse and, 29, 50
   employee-assistance programs
      and, 89
Access control, 105, 106–109
   photo identification badges and,
      106–107, 108
   physical barriers and, 105
   registration logs, 108, 109
Accidents and injury signs of drug
      misuse, 25
Aggravated assault, 19. *See also*
   Assault
Aggressive behavior, dealing with,
      117–122
   body language at meeting for, 120–
      121
   break in the meeting for, 121
   changes in behavior during meet-
      ing for, looking for, 122
   employee-assistance program refer-
      ral and, 122
   employee talking at meeting for,
      121–122
   fear and, 117–118
   keeping meeting focused and, 120
   meeting room for, 118
   security officer's presence at meet-
      ing for, 119–120

seating arrangement for meeting
   for, 120
third party at meeting for, 119
Alarm(s). *See also* Duress alarm
   accidental activation of, 147–148
   duress type of, 109–110, 140, 143,
      144, 145, 147–148
   linkage of, 109
   panic type of, 109–110
   training about, 68
   where to install the, 109
Alcohol abuse in workplace, 50
   absenteeism and, 23
   accident rate and, 23
   crimes associated with, 21
   documentation of employees using,
      30–31
   drivers and, 21, 22–23
   economic cost of, 21
   employee-assistance programs and,
      88, 94
   industrial fatalities and injuries
      and, 23
   monitoring employees using,
      30–31
   performance problems and, 23, 29
   posttraumatic stress and, 163
   screening applicants for, 79
   sickness benefits and, 23
   training to detect symptoms of, 21
Alcohol- and substance-abuse policy,
      23, 28
American Medical Association and
      domestic violence, 32